BY MEGAN DALLA-CAMINA

Women Rising
Simple, Soulful, Sacred
Getting Real About Having it All

SHE WHO REMEMBERS

SHE WHO REMEMBERS

Awakening feminine wisdom in a
world ready for her return

MEGAN DALLA-CAMINA

Published 2026 by The Kind Press

Copyright © Megan Dalla-Camina Pty Ltd 2026
The moral rights of the author have been asserted.

This book is copyright. No part of this publication may be reproduced, stored in a retrieval system, or transmitted in any form or by any means, electronic, mechanical, photocopying, recording or otherwise, without prior permission of the publisher.

The Kind Press also publishes its books in a variety of electronic formats and by print-on-demand. Some content that appears in standard print versions of this book may not be available in other formats.

Cover design by Christa Moffitt, Christabella Designs
Author photo © Nick Leary
Typeset in Adobe Garamond Pro by Post Pre-press Group, Brisbane

A Cataloguing-in-Publication entry for this book is available from the National Library of Australia.

ISBN: 978-1-7642476-1-0 Paperback
ISBN: 978-1-7642476-0-3 eBook

Honouring Lineage and Wisdom

This work honours the many spiritual, cultural, and ancestral lineages that have carried feminine wisdom across time. References to figures and traditions are offered with reverence and gratitude, not as interpretations or claims of authority. The feminine is understood here as an archetypal intelligence rather than a gendered identity, expressed through diverse cultures, perspectives, and lived experiences.

For my mother
For my grandmothers
For my sisters
For my teachers.

And for every woman who has ever forgotten her power.
May you remember.

Table of Contents

Preface: To She Who Remembers   xiii

Part One: The Call
1. The Threshold   3
2. The Wisdom We Forgot   13
3. She Who Was Silenced   21
4. When the Old Ways No Longer Hold   29

Part Two: The Remembering
5. Intuition Is Feminine Intelligence   39
6. Presence Over Performance   48
7. Coming Home to Wholeness   56
8. Embodiment Is Power   64
9. The Wisdom of Seasons   72

Part Three: The Return
10. Trusting What You Know   83
11. Living the Feminine Way   92
12. Leading From Your True Self   101
13. Walking With the Goddess   110
14. The Sacred Thread   118

Final Invocation: A Call to Devotion   128

Living Feminine Wisdom:
Companion Practices for She Who Remembers   137

1. The First True Step   141
2. Your Body's Wisdom   145
3. A Remembrance Ritual   149
4. What No Longer Fits   153
5. Beneath the Noise   157
6. The Power of Presence   161
7. Coming Home to Yourself   165
8. Returning to the Body   169
9. Honouring Your Seasons   173
10. Your Inner Compass   177
11. Living From Within   181
12. Leading From Your Centre   186
13. Meeting the Divine Feminine   191
14. The Sacred Circle   195

Keep Returning   200

A Final Blessing   203

She Who Remembers Circles   209

About the Author   211

Your wisdom was never lost.

Only forgotten.

It's time *to remember.*

Preface

To She Who Remembers

There is a knowing inside you.

Maybe it's soft and quiet, like a whisper you hear when the world finally goes still.
Maybe it rises like a fire in your belly, when you feel the urging of *no more*, or *not this*.
Maybe it comes in a dream. Or it lingers as the ache in your chest that won't go away.
Maybe you don't have words for it yet, but you know it. You feel it. Somewhere deep in your soul.

This book is written for that part of you.
The part of you that remembers.

She remembers what it feels like to live from her body, not just her mind.
She remembers how to trust her intuition, even when the world taught her not to.
She remembers that wisdom isn't something to acquire, but something she already carries.
She remembers that success without soul is a kind of exile.

She remembers who she was before the world made her forget.
She remembers the sacred.
And she wants to live from that place again.

We live in a culture that rewards disconnection, especially for women. Disconnection from our truth. Our cycles. Our softness. Our rage. Our rest. Our depth.

We're taught to override, to achieve, to endure. To do it in silence. To do it without complaint.

But feminine wisdom speaks in a different language.
It's not louder.
It's *deeper*.

This isn't a self-help book. It's not a ten-point plan. It's not a promise that if you do more, everything will fall into place.

This is *a remembering*.

Of who you are beneath your roles. Of what you know beyond your credentials. Of how you were meant to move through the world, before the world taught you to shrink, to be small, to be silent.

It's a manifesto.
And it's also a prayer.

A map. A mirror.
A *threshold*.

Because something ancient is awakening in women right now.

And we are not here to rise by becoming who or what the world told us to be.

We are here *to return*.

To the wisdom that was always ours. To the rhythm we have carried for generations. To the embodied intelligence of a life led from within.

To the feminine wisdom that is your birthright.
It's where you belong. It's where you are home.
It's where both your peace and your power reside.

And it's time for you to remember.
To return to all that is true and sacred.
And to leave behind everything that is not.

May this book be your companion on that return.

And may it light the fire of this truth within your soul:

Your wisdom was never lost.
Only forgotten.
It's time to remember.

PART ONE

The Call

The world may not understand your longing.
But your soul does.
This is not just the beginning of your journey.
It's the threshold of you answering the call.

The call to remember.
The call to return.
The call to rise.

You don't need to have it all figured out.
You only need to take this next true step.
And trust that it will *lead you home*.

Chapter One
The Threshold

There comes a moment, often quiet yet unmistakable, when the life we've built no longer fits the truth we carry.

Maybe you know that moment.

Maybe you've been living inside of it for a while.

It doesn't always arrive with fireworks or fanfare. More often, it comes wrapped in the ordinary: your calendar is full, your days are accounted for, the world sees you as competent, composed, maybe even successful. You're doing everything right.

But inside, something is stirring. A hum. A restlessness. A soft ache tugging at your attention.

You try to brush it off, but it keeps finding you. In the silence. In the quiet knowing that something is shifting, and you can't unfeel it.

It's the knowing that you've outgrown what you were taught to value. That success without soul eventually feels like self-betrayal. And that you're being called somewhere deeper, even if you don't have the name or the map for it yet.

This is not a breakdown. Though it may feel like it.

It may feel like your world is falling apart or you've lost the parts of yourself you were always sure about. It might feel like you no longer know who you are or what you want or what you are here for.

This is not the time to go back to sleep, though you may want to.

But this is not a crisis.

It's a threshold.

And you are standing at its edge.

A world between stories

If you've felt disoriented lately, like the ground beneath you is shifting, it's not just you.

We are in a time between stories, between paradigms, between ways of being. The systems and values that have shaped our culture for centuries are cracking under their own weight.

Productivity has become pathology. Disconnection is dressed up as success. The metrics we once relied on to guide our lives – achievement, status, speed – are no longer enough. As if they ever were.

Many of us are grieving and we don't even have language for it.

We're grieving the way we've had to perform to belong. We're grieving the parts of ourselves we silenced to fit in. The wildness we tamed. The stillness we've sacrificed at the altar of doing. The wisdom we learned to ignore in order to survive. The parts of ourselves we had to abandon just to make it through.

And while that grief may be invisible to the world, it lives in our bodies.

In the clenched jaw. The tired eyes. The bone-deep weariness we carry.

But beneath the grief, something else is stirring.

Something ancient.

A collective remembering is underway. A sacred kind of uprising.

It's not loud and visible, but quiet, embodied, and rooted in truth. It's happening in kitchens, in meditation rooms, in therapy sessions, in journal pages, in circles of women gathering under new moons and around dining tables. It's happening in boardrooms and birth rooms, classrooms and corridors of power, often quietly, often unseen.

But it is happening.

The feminine is rising.

And with it, a wisdom that the world has forgotten but desperately needs. *Especially now.*

We were taught to forget

Let's name it clearly: this forgetting was never accidental.

Feminine wisdom, the embodied, intuitive, relational, cyclical, was once revered. It was the domain of priestesses, medicine women, seers, midwives, and mystics. It was central to how communities lived, made decisions, healed, and stayed in rhythm with life and nature.

But over time, that wisdom was erased.

Not by nature, by systems. Patriarchy, colonisation, capitalism, religion. Systems that sought control and domination over women and anything that threatened their hold on power.

And what women were taught began to change.

We were taught that knowledge lives in books rather than in our bodies.

We learned to see power as force when in truth it lives in being.

We were told that our worth was measured in what we did instead of in who we are.

That leadership is about command, not care. That intuition is naive. That emotion is weakness. That softness is a liability. That *being a woman* is a liability.

Women were taught to suppress their knowing, their cycles and their magic. We were conditioned to be pleasing, perfect, and palatable. We learned to shape-shift. To make ourselves small so we could belong. We were taught to conform and fit in not just to succeed, but to survive. We learned to fear our own power and mistrust our own voices.

But deep down, we've always known our truth.

Even if we didn't have the words for it.

Even when we've doubted it.

Even when it got buried beneath burnout and busyness and trying to be all things to all people with nothing left for ourselves.

There is a part of you that has never forgotten.

And now, *she is ready for her rebirth.*

The invitation

Thresholds are not places of comfort. They are places of initiation.

In myth, the threshold is where the heroine meets her moment. Where she steps beyond the familiar into the unknown, into the heroine's journey. Where the old self sheds and something more whole is born.

You may not know what you're stepping into.

But you do know that *you can't go back*.

This is not a time to numb out or bypass.
It's not a time to push through.
It's a time to feel what's rising.
To listen for what's calling.

To pause long enough to ask:
What am I really here for?
What is no longer true for me?
What have I pretended not to know?
What if the life I want isn't built through striving, but through surrendering?

Thresholds rarely offer certainty. But they do offer truth. And truth is where feminine wisdom lives.

A different way of knowing

Feminine wisdom is not a gendered concept. It's not about patriarchal ideas of femininity or gender norms. It's embodied intelligence – a way of knowing and being that is rooted in the body, in intuition, in emotion, in relationship and rhythm.

It's the wisdom that lives in the pause. In the spaces in between. In the way your body tenses before your mind can explain why. In the deep exhale that follows a truth you finally name.

Feminine wisdom says:
You are not a machine.
You are not behind.
You are not broken for feeling what you feel.
You do not have to choose between power and peace, ambition and alignment.

This wisdom is not performative.
It's not loud.
It's not for sale.
It's sacred.
And it belongs to you.

You were never meant to do this alone

One of the greatest lies of modern life is the myth of individualism, that we must figure it all out by ourselves. But feminine wisdom is relational. It remembers the power of circles, of stories, of shared experiences.

You are not meant to carry your awakening alone.

You are not weak for wanting support, spaciousness, or slowness.

You are wise in your longing for depth.

Let that longing lead you. Let the ache guide you home. Let this book be your companion as you cross the threshold and begin again.

Not by reinventing yourself, but by *remembering yourself.*

You are the beginning

If you're here reading this, then something in you already knows.

Maybe your life looks full but isn't fulfilling.

Maybe you've hit all the milestones but feel spiritually malnourished. Maybe you're successful but tired, yearning for space to exhale and feel.

Maybe you've been whispering to yourself: *surely there must be more than this.*

Maybe that hope has become your daily prayer.

Or maybe you've already begun. Maybe you're remembering. Maybe you've stopped pretending and started listening.

Whatever brought you here, it was not a mistake.

The feminine doesn't ask you to be someone else. She asks you to become *more fully yourself.*

She brings you back to the ground of your being.
To the power in your breath.
To the rhythm of your body.
To the truth in your bones.

This isn't self-help.
It's *soul remembrance.*

And it begins here. At this threshold. Right now.
With your courage to pause. To listen and to trust.
With your willingness to release and return.

You don't need to know the whole path.
You just need to take the next true step.
Let this be it.

Chapter Two
The Wisdom We Forgot

There is a kind of knowing that doesn't live in books or theories. It lives inside you.

In the pause before a decision. In the tightening of your body when something is off. In the patterns that repeat until you finally listen. In the feeling you get around certain people before a word is even spoken.

In the way you know when something is meant for you, even if no one else understands why.

That is feminine wisdom. And for too long, we were taught not to trust it.

So much so that *we forgot we even had it.*

What we were told

We were taught that real knowledge is empirical, quantifiable, logical. We were taught to prioritise reason over feeling. Data over intuition. Head over heart. We were taught to distrust what we couldn't measure.

We internalised the belief that the instinctual was suspect, or at best, secondary. That wisdom should be external and credentialed. That it should sound a certain way, come only from sanctioned sources, fit inside approved systems. And if it didn't, it wasn't credible.

So, we looked outward so that we would be taken seriously.

We sought the experts. The formulas. The ten steps and the clear paths. We read the books, signed up for the courses, attended the workshops, collected the accolades. We followed the rules until we were drained and exhausted.

And yet, even as we accumulated knowledge, many of us felt further away from our knowing.

We got the data, but we forgot *the devotion*.

Because we were bypassing the wisdom within.

What feminine wisdom is

Feminine wisdom isn't a style or aesthetic. It's not about performing softness. It's not about being agreeable and graceful, or endlessly accommodating.

And it's not about swinging to the other end of the spectrum and rejecting structure, logic, or ambition.

Feminine wisdom is a deep, ancient, embodied way of knowing. It's rooted in relationship: to self, to spirit, to earth, to each other. It honours the cyclical nature of life, the intelligence of emotion, and the depths of our intuition.

It doesn't move in straight lines. It moves in spirals, through seasons and symbols. It reveals itself through rhythm, reflection, ritual, and rest.

This wisdom lives in your body, not just your brain. In your ability to take a deep breath, not just fill your calendar. In your ability to revitalise your energy, not just push your output. In your capacity to feel, not just your ability to prove.

It doesn't arrive in commands. It arrives in whispers and signs, in deep inner knowing.

Feminine wisdom invites us to listen for what's beneath the words. To follow what enlivens us. To trust what is felt, not just what is seen or can be proven. To remember that truth doesn't have to be defended to be real.

It's not either/or.
It's both/and.
The inner and outer. Visible and invisible. Mystical and practical. Known and unknown.

And it belongs to all of us.

How it was lost

The forgetting didn't happen all at once. It happened slowly. Systematically.

Across generations, feminine ways of knowing were dismissed, devalued, and often deliberately destroyed.

In ancient cultures, the feminine was revered. She was embodied in goddesses, priestesses, healers, and wisdom keepers. Women held the medicine. They were the guardians of birth and death, the ones who attuned to the unseen, and walked between worlds.

But as patriarchal systems solidified, that power was recast as dangerous. Intuition became hysteria. Wisdom became heresy. Embodiment became shame. Healing became witchcraft. And along with it, the feminine became suspect.

What couldn't be controlled was silenced. What couldn't be understood was labelled irrational.

What couldn't be dominated was called wild and untrustworthy. And women were punished for it.

Witch trials. Colonisation. Religious dogma. Scientific reductionism. These forces didn't just marginalise women. They severed humanity's relationship with *the feminine itself.*

As women, we internalised this disconnection.
We forgot the uniqueness of our rhythms.
We suppressed what made us feel most alive.
We learned to distrust the very wisdom that was meant to guide us.

But wisdom cannot be extinguished.

It lives on.
In our bodies.
In our dreams.
In our lineage.
In our essence.

The return begins within

To reclaim feminine wisdom is not to reject masculine energy or intelligence. We need both. We *are* both. What we are seeking is balance and integration. A return to wholeness.

But that balance begins with reclaiming what has been missing. Healing what has been wounded, and reawakening what has been silenced.

This is not about becoming someone new.
It's about becoming more you than you've ever allowed yourself to be.

And that begins with remembering:

Your body is wise.
Your emotions carry intelligence.
Your cycles are sovereign.
Your intuition is your compass.
Your longing is your map.

Feminine wisdom isn't something to master, it's something to re-enter. Something to attune to and practice, without need for perfection.

You remember by listening. By noticing. By heeding the voice within that says:
This matters.
This doesn't.
This is for me.
This is not.

The feminine doesn't demand. She invites.
She doesn't force your transformation.
She holds space for it.

This is devotional work

Reclaiming feminine wisdom is not a lifestyle trend or personal development goal.

It's sacred work.
It's ancestral work.
It's healing work.

It's also cultural repair. Because when one woman remembers, it changes everything.

Feminine wisdom doesn't stay confined. It ripples. Into how we lead. How we parent. How we love. How we create. Into how we show up in rooms, in relationships, in rituals, *in resistance*.

This isn't just about empowerment.
It's about *embodiment*.

And it's about returning: to yourself and to the truth that you don't need fixing or saving. You simply need to remember the depths of who you already are.

So let this be your invitation.
To pause.
To feel.
To question.
To begin again.

To trust that what lives within you is enough.

To know that your body is not a barrier, it's a bridge home to yourself.

To understand that wisdom doesn't have to be explainable to be real.

To remember that you don't have to earn your worth.

You already are the wisdom you seek.

You are She Who Remembers.
And you are not late.
You are right on time.

Chapter Three
She Who Was Silenced

There are voices that were never truly lost. But they were silenced. Stories were rewritten. Power was erased. And truth was buried beneath centuries of fear.

Let's be very clear: she was silenced not because she lacked wisdom, but because *she carried too much of it.*

Not because she was small, but because she was so vast she could not be controlled.

Not because she was wrong, but because she remembered something the world wanted to forget.

She was the priestess. The prophet. The poet.
The healer, the rebel, the mystic. She spoke the language of the divine, and for that, they tried to bury her.

But just because she was silenced doesn't mean she disappeared.

She remains in the deeply buried parts of us. In our DNA. In our psyche. In our blood and in our bones. In the longing to remember what we know in our soul we have been missing.

There's a silence that lives inside history. A silence filled with names not spoken, stories not told, and wisdom forgotten.

But just because something has been silenced doesn't mean it's gone.
Some truths go underground.
They become part of the soil.
They become seed.
They wait.
Until the ground is fertile.
Until it's time.

And now, they are rising.

Across centuries and cultures, women have carried wisdom in their souls. They carried it quietly, often dangerously. They remembered the sacred in the everyday. They kept time with the moon. Healed with their hands and their hearts. Spoke in symbols, ancestral memory and stories, dreams and bloodlines.

And many got trapped in a culture and time of feminine erasure.

Not because they weren't powerful.
But because they were.

Mary Magdalene and the power of misremembering

Mary Magdalene was one of them. You may know her by name. But what you've heard is probably not the truth.

She wasn't a repentant prostitute.
She was a teacher. A mystic.
The apostle to the apostles.
In some texts, the one He trusted most.

She stayed when others fled.
She witnessed what others couldn't.
She understood what others missed.
She taught the truth and the way.

But her power and position didn't fit the story they wanted to tell. So, they rewrote her. They changed her story to reduce and diminish her. And in the process, they demonised her, which was their very intention.

For two thousand years, she was remembered not for her wisdom, but for the shame they cast upon her.

And yet, the truth of who she was persisted. In hidden gospels. In symbols. In the red thread of remembrance passed through time, from woman to woman, believer to believer.

Mary Magdalene is more than a figure in history.
She's an archetype of what has been forgotten
about the feminine that is now being reclaimed.

She is the voice inside you that says:
Something is missing here.
There is more to this story.
There is more to me.
And we must remember.

They were always here

Mary is not alone.

There was Enheduanna, high priestess of ancient Mesopotamia, the first recorded author in human history.
There was Hildegard of Bingen, the medieval mystic, composer, poet, visionary, and founder of her own convent.
There was Mirabai, Bhakti saint and Hindu rebel poet who chose devotion to Krishna over duty, even when it meant exile.
There were the wise women of Europe, persecuted as witches for their plant medicine and their knowing.
There were African priestesses and Indigenous grandmothers, whose songs and stories kept the world in rhythm long before it was mapped by men.

There were countless others.
Some known. Many forgotten.
All part of lineages that refused to die.

It's critical to understand that they didn't just disappear; they were buried under soil, and under systems.

Systems that feared what they could not control.
That shamed what they could not understand.
That punished what they could not dominate.

And yet, their wisdom lives on.
In our bodies. In our dreams.
In the ache we feel when we know something isn't right.
In the knowing that rises when we know that it is.

The cost of forgetting

When we forget these voices, we forget part of ourselves.

We forget that wisdom can be felt, not just proven. That knowing can be cyclical, not only linear. That we are worthy simply because of who we are, not because of what we do.

We forget that we come from women who created worlds and walked between them. Who honoured death as part of life. Who saw beauty as prayer, and rest as medicine.

We forget that feminine wisdom was once central, not marginal. Revered, not dismissed. Trusted, not ridiculed.

And in all of that forgetting, we have paid a high price. A price that only women have been asked to pay.

We see it in the epidemic of burnout. In the suspicion of softness. In the disconnection from our bodies, from the earth, and each other.

We see it in the way women doubt themselves even when they know. In the mistrust of other women. In the way we shrink ourselves to make others comfortable. In the way we apologise for our needs, our feelings, our truth, our depth.

But there is a path forward.

Because this forgetting is *not the end of the story.*

Remembering as rebellion

To remember is not nostalgia.
It's rebellion.
It's repair.

When we speak their names, we don't just remember forgotten women. We reclaim something that has always been ours. We remind ourselves that we come from a lineage of women who knew. Who felt. Who healed. Who led through devotion, not domination.

You may not have been taught their stories in school.
But your body remembers them.
Your soul remembers them.
And *they remember you.*

No matter where you're from, you are part of this lineage.

Not because you've studied it, but because you are living it.

Every time you trust your intuition.
Every time you choose resting over racing.
Every time you speak what others won't.
Every time you witness the mystery in the ordinary.

You remember.

You live what they lived until they could not.
You carry forward what they began.
You add your voice to the song that was never meant to be silenced.

The feminine is not a concept. It's a continuum

This isn't about idolising the past. It's about weaving it into the present to create a different future. Bringing the wisdom of those who came before into how we live now.

You don't need to become a mystic or scholar to be part of this return. You only need to hear the call and listen.

There is wisdom in your longing.
There is guidance in your grief.
There is truth in your resistance to what no longer feels right.
The feminine isn't out there.
She's *in here*.
In your breath. Your belly. Your being.
Your becoming.

And she isn't asking for performance or perfection.
She is simply asking for your presence.

This chapter may not come with a map.
But it does come with a memory.
A memory and lineage of women who once walked this path.

You are not alone.
They were always here.
And now, *so are you.*

Chapter Four
When the Old Ways No Longer Hold

There are moments in history when the old ways no longer hold. When what once brought safety and security begins to unravel. When the questions we've been avoiding can no longer be suppressed. When living differently becomes the only real choice.

We are living in one of those moments.

Beneath the busyness of everyday life, there is a quiet revolution underway.

It's not being broadcast but it is being felt. In women's bodies and in their choices. In their refusal to keep performing a version of success that costs them their wholeness.

There is a reason so many women are exhausted. A reason so many are burned out, numbed out, or quietly disillusioned with their life and their lot.

It's not because they're weak.
It's not because they're doing something wrong.
It's because the system is broken.
And deep inside, *we know it.*

The weight of disconnection

For too long, we've been told that our worth lies in what we produce. That we must earn our place by proving our value. That we must keep going, no matter how tired we are. That success comes at the price of rest, of intuition, of softness, of ourselves.

We've been conditioned to override our inner truth in the name of achievement.
To suppress our cycles.
To devalue our emotions.
To mistrust our bodies.
To silence our knowing.

And we've paid the price.

We see it in the rise of anxiety, autoimmune conditions, hormonal imbalances, depletion. We see it in women who are outwardly thriving but inwardly unravelling. We see it in the widening gap between what we do and who we are. We see it in the quiet grief of women who've climbed the ladder only to find it leaning against the wrong wall.

But this is not the end of the story.
It's the beginning of a new one.

Because more and more of us are saying:
Not this.

Not like this.
No more.

The rise of a new way

There is a groundswell of women returning to themselves. They aren't waiting for permission or asking for validation. They are simply choosing to live differently.

They are reclaiming their rhythms.
Tending to their energy.
Centring their wellbeing.
Trusting their intuition.
Rewriting the rules.

They are leading from embodiment, not ego. Choosing aligned impact over empty performance. Allowing softness to be a strength. Building lives that feel good on the inside, not just impressive on the outside.

And in doing so, they are quietly changing not just their world, but the entire world.

This is the power of feminine wisdom: it transforms from the inside out.
It doesn't impose change, it invites it.
It doesn't dominate, it magnetises.

It doesn't fracture, it heals.

This isn't about going backward.

It's about going inward.

Feminine wisdom as cultural repair

The reclamation of feminine wisdom isn't just personal healing. It's a cultural necessity.

Because the systems we've built – political, economic, environmental, technological – are suffering from the same imbalance we see in ourselves:
Too much force, not enough flow.
Too much dominance, not enough dialogue.
Too much extraction, not enough reverence.

We are witnessing the consequences of a world divorced from the feminine. A world that sees the earth as a resource instead of a living being. That values extraction over sustainability. That ignores the wisdom of the land as well as the lineage.

To return to feminine wisdom isn't to reject progress, it's to redefine it. It's to create a future
that honours life in all its forms.

Where the language of leadership is love, not fear.
Where power is rooted in purpose.

Where success includes soul.
Where justice is infused with joy.

The world doesn't need more productivity. It needs more peace. More women who are deeply grounded in themselves. More choices made from abundance, not scarcity. More lives lived in alignment with what truly matters.

A turning point

Feminine wisdom matters now, because we are at a collective turning point. The old model has been revealed for what it is: unsustainable, extractive, performative, exploitive.

We are being invited to choose differently. To pause and to listen.

You don't have to quit your life or abandon your ambitions. Feminine wisdom isn't about withdrawing, it's about realigning. It's about infusing your life with truth. Anchoring your choices in integrity. Living in devotion to what is sacred, both within you and around you.

When you live from feminine wisdom, you don't opt out, you *opt in*. Into a more embodied and expansive way of being.

You become the woman who doesn't need to have it all figured out to take the next step. You trust that your power doesn't live in your proving or productivity but in your attunement, your discernment, your knowing of what is right for you, even if no one else understands it.

This is the leadership the world is asking for.
Not louder. Not faster.
Quieter. Truer. Wiser. And just more honest.

You are being called

You are not here by accident. You are not reading this by chance. You are here because something in you remembers.
Something in you knows there is another way.
And maybe, just maybe, that way begins with you.

With your willingness to trust your body.
To protect your energy.
To say no to what drains you and yes to what enlivens you.
To rest without guilt.
To lead without leaving yourself behind.
To believe that your softness is strength, that your truth is to be honoured, that your wisdom is enough.

In fact, it's what matters.

It's what heals.

This isn't just a personal healing, it's a collective awakening.
And it begins now.
With the quiet, revolutionary act of choosing to remember.
Of choosing yourself.

PART TWO

The Remembering

You followed the call.

Now it's time to remember.

Not who the world told you to be, but the woman you have always been.

You are not lost.

You are *remembering*.

The deeper truth.

The ancient rhythm.

The part of you that was never broken ... *only buried*.

Chapter Five
Intuition Is Feminine Intelligence

You've always known.

Even when you didn't have proof. Even when you couldn't explain it. Even when the world told you to ignore it. Somewhere beneath the noise, you've known.

It might have arrived as a nagging nudge. A quiet feeling that something was off. Or when you felt a deep yes in your body before your mind could catch up and say no.

You may have called it a gut feeling. A knowing. A pull. A sixth sense. You might have tried to override it so you could appear rational and agreeable.

And perhaps, at times, you've paid the price for not listening. If you're honest with yourself, you probably know that to be true.

This knowing is your intuition. It's not in your imagination, and it's not a side skill. It's not mystical fluff. It's not irrational and it's certainly not naive.

It's intelligence.

Your intelligence.

It's a deep knowledge system within you. A language of truth that lives in your body, that rises from your soul.

And it's one of the most exiled parts of ourselves that we need to reclaim.

The conditioning against knowing

From a young age, we are trained to outsource our knowing.

We're taught to trust authority over instinct. To follow the rules and prioritise the data. To ask for permission. To make decisions that make sense on paper. To override our intuition in the name of logic, or likeability that feels like survival.

We internalise the belief that something isn't real unless it's measurable. That what we feel must be backed by evidence, and it's not true until we can prove it. We are taught that our instincts are unreliable, *especially as women.*

We've been told we're too emotional and that we overreact. That our perceptions are subjective and suspect and we just need to calm down.

And so, we learned to doubt ourselves. To hesitate. To seek endless validation. To analyse instead of trust. To numb out instead of tune in.

This disconnection doesn't just weaken our decisions; it weakens our sense of self.

Because when you no longer trust what you know, you no longer trust *who you are.*

What intuition really is

Intuition is not the opposite of logic. It's not guesswork. And it's certainly not magical thinking.

It's an embodied form of perception, a way of knowing that arises from deep awareness, pattern recognition, emotional intelligence, and energetic attunement.

It lives in the nervous system and the subconscious mind.

In the body's signals, both subtle and strong.

In the space between stimulus and response.

In our learning to respond, not react, so we can tune into our truth first.

It's the wisdom that tells you not to trust someone before they've shown you why. It's the flash of clarity in the middle of the night, or that first thought you have in the morning before your brain switches on.

It's the ache in your chest when you're betraying yourself, before you even realise it. It's the sense of being guided. And it's the long slow exhale of relief when you finally make the right choice for you.

We've been trained to dismiss these cues. But they are sacred, and they are yours.

Listening to the quiet voice

One of the reasons we struggle to hear our intuition is because we've become so accustomed to ignoring it.

We live in a culture of noise, of constant input, distraction and optimisation. It's hard to hear the voice of your inner knowing when you're moving at the speed of productivity.

But intuition doesn't shout.

It whispers, and waits for the moment you are quiet enough to hear it.

That means practising stillness. Releasing the cultivated desire to move at such a fast pace and learning how to live in the pause. In the spaces between.

It means softening the need for external validation, even though we've been conditioned for a lifetime to look for it and crave it.

It means noticing what your body feels around certain people, in certain spaces, and when you're making certain decisions.

Listen in: does your body contract or expand?
Does your breath get shallow, or does it deepen?
Does your energy rise or fall?

Listen.

Your body is wise. And it is always communicating with you.

The calmer our nervous system, the clearer we hear. The more we listen, the louder the signal. The more we follow it, the more it leads us to our truth, guides us to where we need to be, and shows us who we really are.

Reclaiming intuition as feminine technology

Let's name what's radical here: trusting yourself in a world that profits from your doubt is a revolutionary act.

The reclamation of intuition is a return to sovereignty. It's how we stop leaving ourselves behind. It's how we live, lead, love, and create from alignment and abundance rather than fear and scarcity.

This is also about restoring balance to an inner world long skewed toward the masculine.

It's about *inviting the feminine back in.*

We need both the rational and the intuitive. The analytical and the embodied. The logic that defines and the wisdom that guides.

When we lead from both, we remember our wholeness.

When we lead from within, in a way that feels authentic, we hold our power.

Feminine wisdom asks us to return to the part of us that never forgot. To trust our timing. To follow our longing and our knowing. To trust what feels true before it makes sense.

And yes, it will feel uncomfortable at first. Because the world taught you to override it. Because it's easier to follow someone else's formula than to follow your own soul.

But *your soul is calling.*

And she will speak through you if you listen.

A path for returning to your intuition

Here is an invitation.

When you are faced with a decision, *pause.*

Place one hand on your heart, and one on your belly.

Close your eyes.

Take three slow, deep breaths.

Tune in to your body and ask: *What feels true?*

Listen.

You may not get an answer right away and that's okay. It takes time to rebuild trust with your inner voice, especially if you've spent years silencing her.

But she's still there. She always has been.

And the more you listen, the more you'll hear.

Not just because your intuition gets louder, and it will, but also because you've learned to turn down the noise around it.

You've learned to tune in. And you will continue to learn to trust yourself.

Trusting yourself is the first return

This feminine code, this remembering, is not small.

It's foundational.

Because everything that follows in this book, and in your life, requires a relationship with your own inner wisdom.

You cannot reclaim your power without reclaiming your knowing.

You cannot embody your truth while denying your true voice.

You cannot become who you are here to be if you keep betraying what you feel. If you keep betraying *who you are.*

So let this be the moment you stop waiting for certainty. Let this be the moment you begin to trust your own discernment.

Let this be the moment you believe:
You already know.
You always have.
And now, *you get to remember.*

Chapter Six
Presence Over Performance

You've been performing for so long, you might not even realise it. But your body does.

You learned the roles early.
Be polite. Be productive. Be pleasing. Be perfect. Smile. Achieve. Stay busy. Don't take up too much space. Don't make too much noise. Don't step outside the lines. Take care of everyone.

Be a good girl.

You became so practised at playing the part that it became second nature. So meticulous at meeting expectations that you forgot to ask what *you* wanted or expected.

So good at keeping it all together that you forgot what it feels like to fall apart.

We've been taught to wear masks so convincingly that we forget they're even there.

We've become fluent in pretending. That we're fine. That we're fulfilled. That we've got it all under control.

But here's the truth beneath the mask:
You are tired of performing.
Your soul is exhausted.

And presence is what you long for most.

The performance of womanhood

In a patriarchal culture that rewards productivity and perfection, performance becomes survival.

We perform competence at work, even when we're crumbling inside. We perform calm in meetings, even when we long to shout. We perform happiness on social media, even when we're lonely or lost. We perform ambition, because to admit we want something less might mean disappointing someone.

We perform perfection everywhere, keeping up appearances so our entire world doesn't disintegrate.

The performance becomes armour. It keeps us safe and seen. Approved of. But it also keeps us disconnected, from our bodies, our truth, our needs, our joy.

And over time, the cost is high. Too high.

Because the performance isn't just external. It shapes how we see ourselves. We begin to believe that love must be earned. That worth is conditional, and it depends on approval. That we are only as valuable as our output, our likeability, our usefulness, our image.

We become strangers to ourselves.

What is presence

Presence is the antidote. It's the breath-by-breath return to what is here now.

It isn't a strategy; it's a state of being. Not something to achieve, but something you allow.

Presence is the moment you drop the mask.
The moment you feel your feet on the earth.
The moment you breathe all the way down into your belly. The moment you stop bracing for the expected outcome and start softening into what is real.

It's the moment you return to the truth of who you are when no one is watching. And then, *even when they are.*

It's what happens when you stop performing for other people and start belonging to yourself.

It's not always comfortable. Sometimes it reveals the pain we've been avoiding.

Sometimes it brings the truth of how we really feel beneath the numbing, and with it, tears from desire we buried so deep we forgot the longing was even there.

It brings honesty, and that is the gateway home.

Why we fear it

Presence demands our attention. It asks us to feel what's actually here. Not what we wish were here, or what we pretend is here, but what is real.

And *that* can be *terrifying*.

We fear it because it threatens the illusion we've built. It calls out the stories we tell ourselves to stay safe:

"I'm fine."
"This is just the way it is."
"If I slow down, everything will fall apart."
"If I show up as I am, it won't be enough."

And when those stories begin to unravel, it can feel like *we* are unravelling.

But those stories were never true. They were just familiar. And we clung to them because we didn't trust that simply being – without doing, without proving, without performing – was enough.

But you are not falling apart.
You are coming home.

The power in slowing down

Feminine wisdom moves at the speed of the body, not the speed of urgency. It lives in the present moment, not in productivity and pressure.

To return to presence is to reclaim your power. Because when you're present, you can hear yourself. You can feel your boundaries. You can notice the signals your body is sending. You can respond, rather than react.

You no longer say yes when you mean no. You no longer betray yourself just to be liked. You no longer override your needs in the name of someone else's expectations.

Presence isn't passive. It's powerful. It allows you to act from clarity rather than conditioning.

This is the foundation of feminine leadership:
Not what you do, but *who you are*.
Not how much you achieve, but how aligned you are as you achieve.
Not how well you perform, but how deeply you belong to yourself, even in the moments no one sees.

The practice of being

Reclaiming presence requires intention. It's something we practice in devotion and continual realignment.

Try this:

> Before a meeting, a conversation, or a decision, pause.
>
> Breathe.
>
> Place your hand on your heart.
>
> Ask: *Am I here? Am I in my body, present with myself?*

You can do this anytime: while making tea, before checking your phone, while brushing your teeth or walking into a meeting.

Presence lives in the everyday. In the simple moments we so often rush through.

Over time, this living awareness becomes a way of life. And in that space of being, you begin to remember:
You don't need to prove your worth.
You don't need to hold it all together.
You don't need to show up as anything other than who you are.

Your grounded awareness is your most radiant offering. And it's the source of the deepest wisdom you can carry.

Your presence is enough

In a world that rewards doing, producing, and proving, it's easy to forget: your presence is enough.

Not your performance. Not your perfected and polished version. Not the endless tasks you complete or the roles you fill.

Just you here now, breathing, showing up in your truth.

You don't need to have all the answers or hold everything together to be valuable. Sometimes, what's most powerful is your quiet stillness. Your ability to listen, to be the witness. To simply be.

It might feel small, but it's not.

Your energy has impact. Your calm steadiness shifts the room. You being grounded invites others to anchor into themselves too.

You are allowed to stop performing. To take off your mask and to rest, to open up and be seen for who you truly are.

You were not born to meet expectations.

You were born to tell the truth of who you are.
To live inside your body. To be here for your one beautiful life.

You are here to soften into the fullness of who you are.
Not the version that pleases, but the one that belongs.

You don't have to earn your worth through effort.
You don't need to prove your value through perfection. You don't have to people-please your way to acceptance.

You are not here to be everything. You are here to be fully, deeply, and unapologetically yourself.

Your only work is to come home to yourself again and again, as many times as needed.

This is not about performing your healing.
This is about practicing simply being.
One breath and one truth at a time.

Chapter Seven
Coming Home to Wholeness

The world told you to hustle. But your soul is summoning you to come home.

Even though the world teaches us to forget, to leave parts of our truth behind, it's time to remember. You were never meant to live in pieces: fragmented, overextended, all output, no centre.

Yet this is the reality for so many women today. Moving faster than their souls can keep up. Trying to prove their worth by how much they can carry, how much they can produce, how well they can hold it all. How seamless they can make it appear. Oh, and how good they can look while doing it.

Hustle has become the default language of our time.

Be available. Be impressive. Be useful. Be *extra*. There is always more to do.
Something to achieve, fix, manage, or optimise.

It's what we were taught was necessary to survive.

But there is a deeper cost of all this striving: our sense of self.

No – it's more than that.

It costs us *our soul.*

Because hustle culture doesn't just exhaust us, it *fractures us.*

We begin to forget who we are beneath the motion. We slip into a cycle of self-betrayal. We lose access to the quiet inner knowing that says: I am whole, and that is enough.

Feminine wisdom invites us to come back to ourselves. It says: *You don't have to hustle for your worth.* You get to be whole. Just as you are, where you are, right now.

The myth of more

The patriarchy taught us to define success in narrow, linear ways:
Busy became important.
Tired became the new successful.
More became the measure of worth.

But here's what no one tells you: more doesn't always mean better or fuller. Sometimes, it just means more fragmented.

Sometimes we achieve everything we thought we wanted and still feel empty inside. Not because we failed, but because the version of success we inherited was never rooted in wholeness. It was rooted in proving, and it led to disconnection.

We learned to define ourselves by what we do, not by who we are, and in the process, we became strangers to our own rhythm.

Our bodies said slow down.
Our spirit said pause.
But the world said: *stop,* and you will *fail.*
You must keep going.

And so we did. Until we couldn't any longer.

What is wholeness

Wholeness is not perfection. It's not balance as a rigid ideal. It's not having everything neatly figured out.

Wholeness is integration. It's the remembering that you are not just one thing. You are many things, and all of them are sacred.

You are light and shadow.
Power and tenderness.
Grief and joy.
Softness and fire.

Song and silence.

You are the paradox the world needs but rarely makes space for.

Wholeness allows you to stop squeezing yourself into a box that was never meant to contain you.

It allows you to stop pretending. To stop editing yourself for the comfort of others. To stop being perfect and start being present.

It's what happens when you stop trying to be someone you're not and start showing up as all of who you are.

The hustle is not neutral

Hustle culture isn't just exhausting. It's patriarchal, colonial, and capitalist – built on extraction, not reverence. It was never designed to support your body, your cycles, or your wisdom.

The message embedded in hustle culture is clear: you're only as valuable as your output. Rest is laziness. Slowness is weakness. Care is a distraction from productivity.

And for women, that message comes with added layers: excel, but stay composed. Be tireless, but make it look effortless. Achieve, but don't appear too ambitious. If you have a career and children, mother like you don't have a job outside the home.

But feminine wisdom interrupts that pattern.

It asks:
What if your worth was inherent?
What if your energy was sovereign?
What if rest was revolutionary?

The shift: from hustle to alignment

The antidote to hustle isn't doing nothing. It's doing what is resonant. It's moving through life from alignment, not obligation. It's choosing spaciousness over scarcity. It's recognising that your energy is a non-renewable resource and treating it with respect.

This doesn't mean you cast aside your ambitions. It means you allow them to be soul-aligned. It means you choose goals that nourish you instead of deplete you. It means you stop measuring your value by how exhausted you are at the end of the day.

You get to want big things. You also get to want a slower morning, a gentler week, a life that doesn't require you to leave yourself behind.

You get to lead with power and from your essence. To serve others without disconnecting from your own centre. To create change without sacrificing your health, your peace, or your joy.

This is what it means to live from wholeness.

A return to enough

At the heart of this chapter is an important question: What if you stopped trying to be more, and trusted the quiet power of who you already are?

Can you imagine the freedom of no longer proving your value?
Of no longer measuring yourself against output or applause?
Of living from your fullness not your fear?
Of no longer handing your value over to systems that were never designed to support you?

This is how we remember. This is how we return: To the body. To your breath. To the truth of your own wholeness.

The truth is *you are not too much*. You are not too little. You are exactly how you need to be.

And the world needs all of you – not just the polished, productive parts, but the tender, messy, imperfect ones too.

A practice in wholeness

Here's a simple way to begin:

At the end of the day, ask yourself not what you achieved, but instead:

- What did I feel?
- What did I need?
- Where did I listen to myself?
- Where did I abandon myself?
- What could wholeness have looked like today?

Then offer yourself compassion. And begin again tomorrow, from a place of integration.

Because every day you choose wholeness over hustle, you're not just healing yourself. You're healing generations. You're modelling a new way. You're becoming the kind of woman who lives, leads, and creates from her centre, not from her depletion.

You are the medicine

I'm not asking you to quit your life.
I'm inviting you to *inhabit it more fully*.
To bring all of who you are to what you do.

To stop splitting yourself into what you think are acceptable fragments to meet impossible expectations.

Because the truth is that your wholeness is your medicine. It's where healing happens. Not just for you, but for everyone around you.

For your lineage. For our collective daughters. For the spaces you move through and the lives you touch.

Let the hustle go. Let the sacred in. Let your life become a home for all that you are.

And when you forget – because you will – come back to this truth:

You don't need to keep striving to prove your value.

You were born whole.

And you still are.

And now you get to *live from that truth*.

Chapter Eight
Embodiment Is Power

Before we rise, we must remember.

Before we reclaim our power, we must come home to the place we left behind: *our bodies.*

The most radical thing a woman can do in this world is to live fully in her body.

Not just exist in it. Not just tolerate it. Not just manage it. But *inhabit* it. Trust it. Reclaim it as sovereign ground.

But this can be challenging because it's not what we were taught, and it's rarely what was role modelled.

We were taught to scrutinise our bodies, not to trust them. To shape them, shrink them, silence them, shame them. To disconnect from their wisdom in order to fit someone else's idea of beauty, femininity, or what the "ideal woman" looks like.

And so we separated from our bodies, as if they were places we no longer wanted to associate with.

But when we leave our bodies, we leave our power. Because the body is where truth lives. It's where intuition speaks. It's where trauma resides and where healing begins. It's where our feminine wisdom takes root and becomes real.

To return to the body is not just an act of healing.

It's an *act of sovereignty*.

A culture of disembodiment

We live in a world that rewards disconnection. A world that values what you can do more than how you feel, and that cultivates women who are numb and compliant.

From a young age, we're taught to override our bodies: to sit still when we want to move, or to smile when we want to cry. To stay silent when something feels wrong, and to keep going when everything in us is asking us to stop.

We're taught to prioritise external approval over internal truth. We learn to see our bodies as objects to perfect and control, rather than as instruments of wisdom to nourish and respect.

This disconnection is not accidental. It's systemic, and it's part of what makes the exploitation of women possible.

And yet, *the body remembers.*

Even when the mind forgets. Even when the culture denies it. Even when we've spent years ignoring its signals. Even when everything around us insists we cannot trust ourselves.

The body keeps whispering:

Come home.
I'm still here.
And I will not leave you.

Listening through the body

To be embodied is to feel. To notice what is happening inside you in real time. To track the subtle shifts: the tightening, the softening, the impulse, the pause. It is intimacy with yourself.

When you are embodied, you can discern your yes from your no.

You can feel where your boundaries need to be.

You can recognise the difference between fear and truth.

You stop making choices from obligation and start choosing from alignment.

Embodiment lets you reclaim authorship over your life, because it grounds you in your own experience, not in someone else's expectations.

This is power.

Not the kind that dominates, but the kind that knows, and cannot be denied.

Why we leave our bodies

Most of us didn't choose disembodiment consciously. We left because *it didn't feel safe to stay.*

We left when we were shamed or blamed. When we were told our hunger was too much. When our voice was too loud. We left to survive, and to belong. To succeed. Or to protect ourselves.

And for a time, it worked. *But the cost was high.*

Disconnection may feel efficient, but it is not sustainable. It leaves us numb, reactive, anxious, exhausted. It keeps us outside of ourselves, standing at the edges of our experience.

It keeps us from accessing the full range of who we are – our emotion, our expression, our wisdom, our essence.

Coming back to the body can feel uncomfortable at first. But discomfort isn't a sign that you're doing it wrong. It's a sign that you're finally allowing what is real to surface.

And what is real must rise, if it is ever to be healed.

The sovereign body

Your body is not a problem to solve. It's not a project or a commodity. It's not a battlefield. Although it may have long felt like that.

Your body is a *sanctuary*.

A sovereign space of intuition, sensuality, spirit, and soul.

The wisdom traditions knew this.
The mystics knew this.
Our grandmothers and their grandmothers and their grandmothers knew this.

They held the body as a portal to the divine: not separate from spirit, but *a home for it*.

To live in your body with reverence is a spiritual act.
To feel, to sense, to move, to rest.

Your body does not just carry your life.

It *is* your life. And it needs your devotion.

Embodiment as revolution

There is a reason the patriarchy has feared embodied women: because a woman in her body cannot be controlled.

She knows what is true for her. She cannot be gaslit or manipulated. She sets her own boundaries. She listens to her own rhythms. She claims both her pleasure and her power.

A woman in her body is not waiting for permission or performing someone else's script.

She is sovereign.

And that kind of power is not easily taken.

It disrupts systems built on obedience. It unsettles cultures built on women's silence. It refuses to collapse back into compliance.

When women return to their bodies, they return to choice and to freedom. To the kind of authority that comes from within.

This is why embodiment is not just personal.
It's political.

It's cultural.

A woman in her body is *a revolution that cannot be undone.*

And when one woman comes home to her body, she opens the door for us all.

A practice of belonging

Here is a simple way to reconnect:

> Sit or lie down. Close your eyes.
>
> Begin slow, gentle breaths.
>
> Ask: *What do I feel in my body right now?*
> Not what do I *think*, but what do I *feel*?
>
> Try to stay with the sensation without trying to change it. When your attention wanders, gently bring it back to your breath and how you feel.
>
> Stay with the intention to listen to your body without judgement for at least five minutes. You may wish to write down what you notice.

This is the beginning of attuning to yourself, and of rebuilding trust where you may have lost it.

You don't have to force your way into embodiment.

You get to quietly come back. One breath at a time.

You are the temple

You are not just thinking your way through this life. You are sensing. Feeling. Moving. Living through your body.

And your body is not in the way of your wisdom.

It *is* your wisdom.

You don't have to be perfectly healed to come home to yourself.

You don't need to wait until you feel confident or worthy.

You only need to soften into the space you already live in.

You are allowed to begin exactly as you are.

It's time to let your body remember.

You are the temple.
You are the priestess.
You are the wisdom you have been waiting for.

And the more you live in your body, the more you live in your power.

Chapter Nine
The Wisdom of Seasons

There is a rhythm older than time, a wisdom women have always carried, moving through our energy, our emotions and our seasons of becoming.

It doesn't follow a schedule. It follows life. It lives in you. And it's asking you to awaken to it.

Linear time was never made for us.

The calendars we follow, the schedules we obey, and the expectations we carry were built along a straight line: always forward, always upward. A constant demand for momentum, for progress that never pauses.

But the feminine doesn't move in straight lines. She moves in circles and spirals. She moves with the moon and with the tides, with the breath as it rises and falls.

And deep down, you know this.
Your body knows this.
Your soul knows this.
Even when your schedule doesn't.

To live from feminine wisdom is to return to rhythm.

To remember that life is not a performance, but a cycle. That growth is not linear but layered.

That wisdom is not a peak to reach, but a labyrinth to walk again and again.

The myth of consistency

We live in a culture obsessed with consistency. Show up the same every day. Be just as productive, just as energised, just as available as on your best day, regardless of what your body or spirit is actually saying.

This expectation is not just unrealistic. It's inhuman. And it doesn't work for women.

Flowers don't bloom all year. The moon doesn't shine full every night. The tide doesn't only rise. And yet, we are taught to override our own seasons in the name of success.

We judge ourselves for needing rest. We push through exhaustion. We shame our own sensitivity. We call ourselves lazy when we are simply *in winter*.

But winter is not failure. It's where restoration takes place. It's where seeds begin to take root.

To be cyclical is not to be unproductive.

It's to be *alive*.

The wisdom of a woman's seasons

As women, we move through many seasons across a lifetime, each with its own rhythm and energy. And every season holds a unique invitation.

But we are rarely taught to move with these natural transitions. We are taught to be constant. To always be in full bloom. To stay driven, no matter the inner weather.

Yet feminine wisdom lives in cycles that mirror the earth herself.

Each season of a woman's life holds deep intelligence:

- Maiden (Spring): A time of becoming, of curiosity, expansion, exploration.

- Mother (Summer): A time of creation, of nurturing, expression, giving form to what wants to be born.

- Sovereign (Autumn): A time of discernment, of boundaries, inner truth, deeper power.

- Crone (Winter): A time of wisdom, of stillness, surrender, remembrance.

These seasons are not rigid, and they aren't only biological. They live in us in layers. You can move through all four in one month, one year, or an entire lifetime.

The more we awaken to these inner seasons, the more we understand what we need. We are attuned to when we need to rest, when to create, when to speak, when to soften.

We are not machines. We are living, breathing wisdom.

And when we stop forcing ourselves to live as if we are always in summer, always producing, always pushing, we begin to remember what it means to live in harmony with our deeper truth.

Seasons of the soul

It's not just the body that cycles, your inner life does too.

There will be seasons of emergence, where ideas and energy blossom effortlessly.

There will be seasons of harvest and fallow, where work comes to fruition.

There will be seasons of decay, where what no longer fits falls away.

And there will be seasons of stillness, where nothing is clear, and everything is quietly transforming.

We often resist our inner seasons when they don't align to who we think we need to be at a certain time in our lives. Or when our vision doesn't match who the world tells us we *should* be.

We fear the pause. We feel behind when we're not moving. We feel broken when we're grieving or restless. Or when it's just taking longer than we want it to.

But feminine wisdom reminds us:
Stillness is not stagnation.
Void is not absence.
Darkness is not failure.
Silence is not emptiness.
It is all the hallowed ground of becoming.

What if you embraced the season you're in instead of trying to rush into the next?

What if you let the quiet times be uncomfortable and let that be okay?

What if you trusted that your rhythm is not a problem to solve, but a truth to follow?

Reorienting to sacred time

Linear time asks: *What do you have to do today?*

Sacred time asks: *What are you being guided toward today?*

Linear time says: *Hurry.*

Sacred time says: *Breathe.*

Linear time says: *You're behind.*

Sacred time says: *You're exactly where you are meant to be.*

To live in sacred time is to attune to *Kairos* – the Greek word for "deep time," the time of soul, of essence, of rightness.

It's the kind of time you feel when you're fully present: when you're in ritual, walking in the woods, with those you love and cherish. When you're not measuring life by the hour, but by the truth of the moment.

This is the feminine relationship to time: not as a master to obey, but as something to commune with.

It's not about doing less; it's about living from depth – from alignment, awareness, trust, spaciousness, and *surrender*.

A practice of rhythmic living

An invitation to begin here:

> Track your energy across the month: When do you feel most clear, most tender, most creative, most tired?
>
> Notice the moon. In which phase do you feel most powerful, most inward, most alive?
>
> Begin to ask: *What is the season of my soul right now?* Not what it should be, but what it is.

Instead of pushing through, *listen*. Adjust where you can. Let the small choices matter. Let your calendar begin to reflect your inner rhythm.

This is not about striving.

It's about returning to a way of being that moves with, rather than against, the truth of your soul.

Rhythm as an embodiment teacher

The more you live in rhythm, the more you remember: you are not here to be endlessly productive. You are here to be in communion with life – to move with its tides, to honour its pauses, to trust its return. To be aligned with the mystery of it all.

You are not here to bloom constantly. You are here to ebb and rise, to rest and renew. To stay true to the deeper pulse that carries you.

This isn't weakness; it's *wisdom*.

The feminine isn't found in straight lines.
She is found in the spirals, through cycles, through the womb of time.

And when you return to her rhythm, *you return to yourself.*

PART THREE
The Return

You remembered who you are.
Not just in your mind,
but in your bones.

You walked through the forgetting.
You softened into the truth.
You listened beneath the noise.

You came back to your rhythm.
To your knowing, to *your sacred yes*.

Now may you live and embody it.
The quiet power of living from within.

Every breath a devotion.
Every choice a reclamation.

This is *the return*.

Chapter Ten
Trusting What You Know

You've been searching for something. A map, a guide, a sign, a voice to say: *this is the way.*

You've been looking for a teacher. In a book, from a mentor, in a moment that finally makes it all make sense.

We all know what that searching feels like.

But the truth is and has always been this:
You already know.

You don't know it through intellect or well laid out plans. You know it from a much deeper place.

From the part of you that still dreams.
The part of you that aches.
That part that urges you to listen, even when you do all you can to forget.

You know it in the tightening of your body when you're about to abandon yourself.
In the flutter in your chest when you're ready to speak your truth.
In the inhale that deepens and the exhale that lengthens when you choose integrity over approval.

There is a compass inside you.
It may have been covered for longer than you care to recall.
But it has never been broken, and it will never abandon you.

The myth of the external answer

We are trained to seek knowledge outside of ourselves.

From the moment we are old enough to question, we are taught that the answers live elsewhere:

In authority.
In textbooks.
In systems.
In strategies.
In gurus.

In someone who must know better than we do. More than we do. Because we're taught that they are smarter than we are. And yes, *'they'* typically means men.

And so, we become excellent seekers.

We consume. We compare. We gather insight and advice from everyone around us. We read, enrol, follow, imitate.

But so often, the seeking becomes a substitute for trust.
We become so busy learning that we forget to listen.

And somewhere in that spiral of seeking, we start to believe that we are not the authority on our own lives.

We forget that every time we override our knowing to follow someone else's roadmap, we leave ourselves a little further behind.

But the feminine path is not about mastery.
It's about returning to our own knowing.

It's about *coming home to what's already here.*

The feminine art of self-trust

To say *I already know* is not to say *I know everything.*
It is to say: *I trust what is true for me right now.*

It's not arrogance.
It's intimacy.
With yourself.
With your inner wisdom.
With the part of you that has always been tuned to truth, even when you didn't yet have words for it.

Self-trust is not about certainty.
It's about attunement – to your energy, your values, the truth of your yes and the quiet power of your no.

It doesn't mean you never ask for help. But it does mean that you stop ignoring yourself in the search for it.

You start choosing from alignment, not anxiety.
You start feeling the difference between fear and intuition.
You start moving from the grounded confidence that says: this may not make sense to anyone else, *but it feels right to me.*

That is feminine power.
It comes from your deep feminine wisdom.

No one can give it to you.
But you can claim it. Own it.
And believe it for yourself.

Returning to your own authority

Feminine wisdom is deeply personal. It doesn't arrive as universal doctrine. It arrives as *resonance*.

Before you can explain it, you feel it.

It feels like breath – like grace, ease, and belonging in your own body.

It feels like *this is mine*, and *this is true*.
Not because someone told you, but because you feel it in your soul.

When you reclaim your inner authority, everything begins to shift.

You make choices from clarity, not from fear.

You stop explaining yourself to people who were never meant to understand you in the first place.

You let go of perfectionism, because truth doesn't need polish.

You stop asking for permission, and start asking:

What do I want?
What do I know?
What do I need?
What is true for me?

This isn't selfish; it's essential. And from that place of inner integrity, you lead, love, and create in ways that are true to who you are at your core.

Living from your inner authority may appear quiet on the outside, but it's revolutionary within.

It's saying no when you used to say yes.

It's pausing before you explain yourself yet again.

It's choosing rest over productivity, and boundaries over burnout.

It's writing a new story, about who you are, and what you're here to live.

When you trust what you know, you stop asking the world for permission to exist.

You give that permission to yourself.

Let it be simple

We are conditioned to believe that wisdom is complex. That insight must be earned and that transformation must be hard.

But the feminine doesn't require complexity.

She says: *Let it be simple.*
Let it be easy.
Let it be felt.
Let it be true.

We've been taught to fear our own clarity, the quiet confidence that lives beneath our doubt. Because a woman who knows her own truth is not easily controlled. So we were told to doubt, to defer and second-guess, to hand our knowing and our agency away.

But knowing isn't dangerous. It's divine. And trusting yourself is not a rebellion as much as it is a homecoming.

What if you already know what to do?
What to say?
What to release?
What to begin?

What if you're wiser than you think, and more capable than you've ever allowed yourself to believe?

What if the wisdom you seek has been waiting patiently inside you all along?

What if you've always known?

Trusting what you know

This isn't about finding your voice.
It's about trusting that it was always there.

Now, you get to live like a woman who knows.
Because you do.

Try this:

    Sit quietly for a few minutes.

    Place one hand on your body, wherever feels right.

    Ask yourself: *What do I know, beneath the noise?*

    Ask: *Where have I been pretending not to know?*

Ask: *What truth is waiting for my yes?*

You may hear something small.
You may hear something life-altering.
You may hear nothing, and instead feel a shift,
a loosening, a softening toward yourself.

Trust that.

Trust the space it creates.

This is not about being certain.
It's about being in relationship with yourself.

The end of seeking

This chapter, this code of self-trust, is not telling you to stop learning or evolving.

It's not telling you to turn inward and never look out again.

It's simply saying this:

The answers you're looking for?
They are not *out there*.
They're *in here*.

In your body.
In your breath.

In your longings.
In your firm no.
In your quiet yes.
In your resonance.

You are not lost.
You are returning.
And the next step is not to seek harder.
It's to *listen deeper*.

You already know the answers.
Now, you get to *hear them*.

Chapter Eleven
Living the Feminine Way

To live the feminine way is to come home to yourself.

It's not about rules or roles.
It's not about what the world expects.
It's not about perfect routines or polished performance.

It's about living from the inside out.

From the pulse of your body and the rhythm of your breath. From the truth that lives within you, even when it doesn't make sense to anyone else.

The feminine way isn't a checklist or a destination.
It's not something to master or monetise.
It's not about looking soft while living hard.

It's a rhythm.
A relationship.
A devotion to the real.
A daily return to what's sacred, within and around you.

It doesn't look one way

There is no single way to live the feminine path.
It's not one-size-fits-all.

Some women live the feminine way by caring for children in conscious homes.
Others live it in boardrooms, refusing to hustle at the cost of their wellbeing.

Some live it through art. Through slowness. Through protest. Through devotion or prayer.

Some live it loud, at the edges of what's expected.

This is what makes the feminine way so powerful:
It meets you where you are.

You don't have to retreat to the mountains to find it.
You don't need to leave your life or renounce your greatest desires.

You simply choose to live from a deeper place.
To let your being inform your doing.
To let your soul lead your schedule.
To let your body be your compass.

And the best thing is, you don't need to earn it.
Because the way is already within you.

Rhythm, ritual, and relationship

Three anchors support the feminine way: rhythm, ritual, and relationship.

Rhythm is how you live in time.

It means moving with your inner seasons.
Tracking your energy.
Noticing when you need stillness, and when you're ready to expand.

It means aligning your life with your body's wisdom, not trying to force yourself to fit a life that's out of sync (and haven't we all done that?).

Feminine wisdom moves with your cyclical nature.
Not every day will look the same.
Not every week will feel the same.

And that isn't a flaw, as patriarchal conditioning might suggest. It's how women are built.
And it's time we stop overriding ourselves to match a rhythm we were never meant to follow.

Ritual is how you return to presence.

Ritual doesn't have to mean incense and altars, though it can.

It can also mean the way you make tea in the morning.
The way you stretch before bed.
The pause in a meeting, when you tune in before you speak.

Ritual is the art of making the ordinary meaningful.
Of creating containers for your truth to rise.
Of marking time with meaning.

It's less about how it looks, and more about how it grounds you.

It's how you make moments matter.

Relationship is how you stay connected.

The feminine path is not meant to be walked alone.

It lives in community.
In circle.
In honest conversation.
In remembering that we heal and rise together.

It's the pathway of connection –
to yourself,
to other women,
to your beloved,
to those you love,
to the divine,
to the earth.

To live the feminine way is to *reweave the web*.
To refuse the myth of independence and instead remember what it means to belong.

Not just to yourself, but to each other.

Living from alignment, not expectation

The feminine way is not without challenge.

It asks you to make choices that may not make sense to others.
To walk away from things that once defined you.
To say no more often, and yes more honestly.

You will disappoint people.
You will be misunderstood.
You will need to set new boundaries.
You will outgrow identities and containers you once worked so hard to create.

But you will gain something far greater:

Your truth.
Your alignment.
Your homecoming.

Living the feminine way means your inner alignment becomes non-negotiable.

You stop twisting yourself into versions that are convenient for others but a betrayal of yourself.

You stop people-pleasing and perfecting and overriding your body.

You stop chasing timelines or goals that don't match your truth, stop giving yourself away, and stop diminishing your true value.

You start asking:

- What is my energy asking for today?
- What feels nourishing, not just productive?
- What do I need right now?
- If I followed joy, what would I do next?
- What is mine to carry, and what is not?

This is not about living perfectly.
It's about living *honestly*.

What this looks like in daily life

Living the feminine way is not something you add to your to-do list. It's how you move through your life.

It might look like:

- Leaving space in your calendar, not filling every minute.
- Resting through your cycles.

- Beginning your morning with stillness, not external noise.
- Taking a gentle walk instead of pushing through at the gym.
- Honouring a decision that doesn't make sense but feels right.
- Speaking your truth in a room that's not used to hearing it.
- Taking a breath and a pause before a hard conversation.
- Letting yourself cry without needing to fix it.
- Choosing beauty, softness, reverence, even in small moments.

This is the art of living from the feminine.
You do not perform this way of life.
You *become it*.

Anchor in to the feminine

Here is a simple invitation to begin your day in the feminine way:

Before you check your calendar or your phone, pause.

Place one hand on your heart and one on your belly.

Ask: *How do I feel?*

Ask: *What do I need?*

Ask: *How can I honour my wisdom today, even in small ways?*

Let that be your compass.
Let it shape your choices.
Let it determine your pace and give you space for grace.
Let the feminine bring you home.

Let it be a way of life

This isn't a morning practice or a weekend retreat.
It's a *reorientation*.

A coming home to what's real.
A devotion to what is sacred.
A commitment to *live from within*.

And it changes everything.

Because when you live the feminine way,
you don't just feel better.

You become grounded.
Magnetic.
Radiant.
Unshakeable.

Soft heart, straight spine, strong boundaries.

You don't abandon yourself to belong.
You *belong to yourself*, and from that place, *you belong everywhere*.

You become the woman who doesn't need to prove anything.
Who doesn't need to chase or perform.
Who walks through the world with rhythm in her step, knowing in her body, owning her power.

You become the woman you were always meant to be.

And you do it not by becoming someone new, but by *living the truth of who you already are.*

Chapter Twelve
Leading From Your True Self

We've been taught a narrow story about leadership.

That it's about titles.
Authority.
Being in charge.
Having the answers.
Knowing the strategy.
Driving the vision.
Speaking the loudest in the room.

But what if leadership wasn't about volume at all?
What if it wasn't about striving, or dominance, or control?

Because this model – the one we've inherited – was never made for women. It was built in boardrooms and on battlefields, through hierarchies that rewarded power *over*, not power *with*.

And yet, we try to fit ourselves into it.
We contort our intuition into logic.
We shrink our softness to appear strong.
We lead with our heads, while abandoning the wisdom in our hearts.

But there is another way. A truer way. A way that doesn't require you to become someone else to be seen as a leader.

Leadership isn't about being above others.
It's about being anchored in yourself.

Rooted.
Responsive.
Present.
Aligned.

It's how you show up – in a team, a family, a room, a relationship, a moment of truth. Whether you're holding a vision, holding a boundary, or holding someone through change.

When you lead from your true self, everything shifts.

Because authenticity is not performative.
It doesn't seek validation.
It doesn't betray itself in pursuit of acceptance.

Leading from your truth means leading from clarity. With integrity. With your whole, imperfect, embodied self.

And that – more than charisma, more than confidence, more than control – is what the world is aching for now.

The performance of leadership

Most women who step into leadership roles are not taught to lead from their inner truth. They are taught to fit into models that were never built for them.

We're told to be confident, but not *too* confident.
To be strong, but still likable.
To be assertive, but not aggressive.
To lead, but in a way that doesn't make anyone uncomfortable.

So, we shape-shift.
We harden.
We become fluent in the language of professionalism, while hiding our true self.
We learn to project competence, even when we're disconnected.

We succeed on paper, while quietly abandoning our deeper purpose.

And then we wonder why it feels empty.
Why burnout creeps in.
Why our bodies rebel.
Why our joy feels so far away.

We were never meant to *lead like this*.

Because leadership that requires disconnection isn't leadership at all, it's performance.

Leading the feminine way

Feminine wisdom doesn't reject leadership.
It *redefines* it.

It says: you don't have to become someone else to lead. You just have to become *more fully yourself.*

It honours the leader who:

- Listens before she speaks.
- Feels what's happening in a room before responding.
- Leads from calm, not control.
- Knows when to push and when to pause.
- Holds space for complexity.
- Leads with reverence for relationships and emotional intelligence.
- Is willing to not know, and still move forward.

Feminine leadership is relational, not hierarchical.
It's rooted in values, not ego.

It's embodied, not performative.

It leads with both vision and vulnerability.
It trusts the body.
It trusts the process.
It trusts that true impact flows from alignment, not force.

Because leadership doesn't have to be loud to be effective. It just has to be real.

The power of authenticity

When you lead from your true self, you are no longer fragmenting who you are to fit into places and spaces that were not designed for you.

You bring your softness *and* your strength.
Your intellect *and* your intuition.
Your boundaries *and* your compassion.
Your grit *and* your grace.

You lead as a whole human.

And this creates a ripple effect, because authenticity is contagious.
When you lead from it, you give others permission to do the same.
You model a different way.

You show your team, your clients, your community – even your children – that success doesn't have to come at the cost of self.

You become the kind of leader who people trust, not because of what you say, but because of *who you are*.

That is what new power looks like.
The kind that leads not from control, but from wholeness.

And this is how we lead the world home.

Aligned leadership in practice

A woman I worked with once walked away from a leadership role that looked perfect on paper but felt hollow in her body. She was always teetering on the edge of burnout.

She didn't have a new job lined up.
What she had was *clarity*.
And when she followed it, not only did her health return, but so did her joy.
She created something that aligned with her truth.

That's leadership grounded in *feminine wisdom*.

Leading from your true self will look different for everyone. But it always begins with respecting your own energy and values.

It might look like:

- Saying no to a role or opportunity that isn't aligned, even if it looks good on paper.

- Creating space in your day for stillness, not just another commitment.

- Naming your needs clearly, without apology.

- Holding a boundary with grace.

- Letting your team know you're in a winter season – a time of rest, reflection, or inward focus – and modelling what that means.

- Leading from collaboration, not control.

- Trusting your intuition in moments where logic alone doesn't offer the full picture.

- Letting people see the human behind the role.

This isn't weakness.
It's wisdom.
It's self-leadership, and that's where all great leadership begins.

A practice to lead from wholeness

Each morning, ask yourself:

- What do I need to be fully present today?
- Where am I leading from performance, and where can I lead from alignment instead?
- What part of me have I been hiding, and what would shift if I brought all of me today?

Let your leadership become a reflection of your deepest truth, not a reaction to someone else's expectations.

The world needs you whole and true

This moment in time doesn't need more burnout.

It doesn't need more women twisting themselves into versions of men to be successful.

It doesn't need more people checking boxes and hiding behind titles with false claims on power.

It doesn't need more leaders pretending they have it all together.

It needs *you*.
Fully. Honestly. Courageously. Vulnerably.
With your feminine traits and your humanity intact.

Because your energy has the power to shift rooms.
Your alignment has the power to shape culture.
Your wholeness has the power to rewrite what leadership looks and feels like.

This is not small work.
It is critical and urgent.
This is the work of our time.

So if you're standing at a crossroads, trying to decide between success and self, or wondering what you have to give up to lead as your truest self, know this:

You don't have to choose.
You can lead and stay connected.
You can rise and remain rooted.
You can hold power and stay authentic.

And when you do, you show us all what's possible.

Let your leadership be a blessing, an act of living and leading aligned with *who you truly are.*

Chapter Thirteen
Walking With the Goddess

She has many names. Many faces. And countless ways of making Herself known.

Sometimes She comes in silence.
Sometimes through fire.
Sometimes in the moment you finally stop pretending.
Sometimes in the grief you can no longer hold back, or the longing you can no longer ignore.

Sometimes She arrives with no words at all, only a deep knowing that you are not alone, that someone sacred is walking beside you.

She is the Divine Feminine.
She is the Goddess.

She was never gone, only waiting for you to notice that She was here.

To remember that She is not the destination.
She is the return.

She walks with you

Walking with the Goddess is not a metaphor.
It's a remembering.

She is not above you.
She is not outside of you.
She is divinity encoded within you.

She lives in your breath and your body.
She is the wisdom that rises when you stop deferring to everyone else and begin listening to the feminine within.

To walk with Her is to walk in devotion, not to something external, but to your inner truth.
It's not about subscribing to a new dogma.
It's about recognising that the sacred was never far away.
It's about honouring the holy as something real and tangible in your own life, in your own being, not just in temples or textbooks.

You don't have to go anywhere to be with Her.
You belong to Her, and *She belongs to you.*

Beyond the pedestal

Some of us were taught to revere the feminine as a concept, something beautiful to admire or romanticise.

But relationship with the Goddess is not about appearance.

It's not something to curate or keep at a distance.
It's not about performing divinity or perfecting your spirituality.

Walking with the Goddess isn't about perfection.
It's about intimacy. About connection.

It's showing up, day after day, even when you feel unsure, tired, or unworthy.

She is not asking you to become holy.
She is asking you to become whole.
She is not asking you to please Her or perform for Her.
She is asking you to *walk beside Her*.

This is the shift:
From worshipping Her on a pedestal to welcoming Her at your kitchen table.
From keeping Her in the temple to letting Her shape your days, your choices, your rhythm, the way you move through the world.

She is not somewhere else.
She is in how you rise each morning.
How you soften instead of push.
How you choose rest rather than reaching.
How you speak your truth, even when your voice trembles.

The many faces of the Goddess

The Goddess doesn't come in a single form.
She is not one thing.
She is not linear, tame, or bound by doctrine.
She is multiplicity, a mystery in motion.

And when you call Her, She comes.

She may arrive as Kali, when you're ready to burn it all down.
As Quan Yin, when the only healing left is compassion.
As Saraswati, when your voice finds its rhythm again.
As Mary, when your heart breaks open wide enough to hold the world.
As Durga, when your boundaries are drawn and your courage ignites.
As Brigid, when you tend the flame of your own becoming.
As Lakshmi, when you open to beauty, radiance, and abundance.

She is Black Madonna. She is White Buffalo Woman.
She is the rose in bloom, and the wildfire that clears the path.
She is the river's flow and the echo of a drumbeat.
She is both the silence and the sound.

You may meet Her through lineage, through dream, through symbol or in the quiet knowing that has no name. She is found in the ordinary places too, in laughter, in laundry, in your long walk home.

You don't need to name Her to know Her.
You don't need to choose one face.
You only need to listen.

She will know the essence of what your soul needs.

She will *meet you there.*

Living as Her vessel

To walk with the Goddess is to remember:
You are not a machine of doing.
You are a vessel of becoming.

You were never meant to strive your way to grace.
You were made to be moved by it, to live in it.

Let your hands be Her hands.
Let your breath be Her breath.
Let your yes be Her prayer.
Let your body become Her altar.

When you walk with the Goddess, you don't transcend life, you consecrate it.

You bring Her into boardrooms and school runs.
Into your grief and your protest.
Into your boundaries, your parenting, your activism, your art.

You bring Her into the moment you forgive yourself.
Into the moment you stop hiding.
Into the moment you remember: *I am not alone.*

And in doing so, you become a living, breathing expression of the sacred.

She lives through you

The Goddess lives in the body. Not just the symbolic body, but your actual, physical body.

In the curve of your hips.
In the blood that moves with the moon.
In the heat that rises when you speak what's true.
In the exhaustion that whispers *it's time to rest.*

To walk with Her is to inhabit yourself again.
To return to sensation. To softness. To the language that only your body knows.

It's a reclamation of what the world once taught you to mistrust:
Your desire.
Your hunger.

Your anger.
Your intuition.

The body is not an obstacle to overcome.
It is a temple of Her wisdom.
A carrier of Her codes.

When you begin to trust your body again – not just when it's performing or pleasing or looking a certain way, but in all Her seasons and cycles – you begin to hear Her voice more clearly.

She speaks in the goosebumps on your skin.
In the butterflies in your stomach.
In the tears you didn't know you were holding back.

Walking with the Goddess isn't about ascending beyond the body.

It's about descending fully into it.

Because your body is not separate from your spirit.

Your body is *where She lives*.

Walking together

A gentle invitation:

Before beginning your day, place your hands on your heart.

Ask: *Who is walking with me today?*

Ask: *What face of the Goddess is needed for what I must meet?*

Ask: *How can I honour Her in the way I move, speak, and rest?*

There is no right way.
Only honesty. Only practice.
Tuning in, holding reverence.

It's the willingness to keep showing up, again and again, in devotion.

You are not walking alone.
You never were.
She is beside you.
She is within you.
She is the part of you that remembers you are already whole.

You walk with Her.
And *She walks with you.*

Chapter Fourteen
The Sacred Thread

Perhaps this began as a personal search.
About your body.
Your exhaustion.
Your aching questions.
Your quiet longing.
Your deep desire for another way.

And it is.
But it's also a doorway into something much bigger.

Because when one woman remembers, the world begins to shift.
When one woman reclaims her voice, generations begin to heal.
When one woman chooses wholeness over hustle, softness over performance, sovereignty over sacrifice, she changes the field around her.
And with that, she changes the world.

This work is deeply personal.
But it is never only personal.

Feminine wisdom doesn't move in straight lines.
It moves in circles.
It spirals. It remembers. It returns.

And every time you say yes to your own truth, you are saying yes on behalf of so many others who are still learning to find their own.

Healing the thread

We carry stories that are not just ours.
We carry our mother's silence.
Our grandmother's sacrifice.
The untold stories of our lineages.
The pain that was swallowed.
The power that was punished.
The wisdom that was buried for safekeeping, waiting for someone brave enough to unearth it.

That someone is you.

You are not just healing your own patterns.
You are weaving a new thread into the collective story.
You are remembering what your ancestors once knew, and what our collective daughters will one day inherit.

You carry more than your own longing, and you rise for more than yourself.

You rise with your mother, and her mother before her.
With the women who were silenced so you could speak.
With the ones who burned so you could remember.

With the ones who endured, so you could choose differently.
You rise because of them.
And you rise for the ones still to come.

Your becoming is not solitary.
It is a continuation.

Every choice you make to live differently, more honestly, more rhythmically, more whole, creates a break in the ancient chain.

And in that space, *something new can begin.*

Sacred activism begins within

It's easy to feel overwhelmed by the scale of what's broken in the world.
The extraction.
The speed.
The injustice.
The grief.

The systems that were never built to hold our humanity.

And yes, we need change.
We need action.
We need voices raised, policies rewritten, old paradigms dismantled.

Now, if not sooner.

But we also need women who are rooted.
Women who are not replicating the same power structures in different forms.
Women who aren't burning out in the name of service.
Women who don't disconnect from their own bodies while trying to heal the world.

Feminine wisdom is a form of sacred activism.

It begins inside you, in how you move through each day.
In how you treat your body.
In how you tend the earth beneath your feet.
In how you see and support other women, not as competition, but as *sisters*.

And from that grounded place, your life becomes a quiet revolution.

Becoming the prayer

The world doesn't change just because we shout louder.
It changes when we come back into right relationship, with ourselves, each other, the earth, and the divine.

This kind of change is slower.
It's less dramatic.
It doesn't always look impressive.

But it lasts.

Because it's built on alignment rather than urgency.
On devotion rather than projection.

So yes, keep building your vision.
Keep speaking your truth.
Keep showing up for what matters.

But do it in a way that reflects the values you want to live.
Let the means reflect the end.
Let your being shape your doing.
Let the way you walk reflect the world you're here to recreate.

Because you are not just a woman with a mission.
You are a living prayer.
You are a living embodiment of the new world we are reimagining.

When you rise, we all rise

Your healing is not a luxury.
Your joy is not frivolous.
Your rest is not laziness.
Your wholeness is not a side project.

These are forms of *resistance*.
Acts of remembrance.

Ways of reclaiming what was once forgotten.

And they matter, not just for you, but *for all of us*.
Because we are interconnected.
Woven.
Tied together by something ancient, sacred and unseen.
Every time you return to your body, you give another woman permission to do the same.
Every time you honour your rhythm, you shift the collective pace.
Every time you choose alignment over approval,
you create space for others to be true.

You may never know the full ripple of your becoming.
But it is real.
And it's unfolding, within you and around you, right now.

A collective practice

You do not have to carry the whole world.
But you can hold your piece of it with reverence.

Think of one way your own remembering might serve others today.

It could be how you show up in a conversation.
How you model rest for your children.

How you speak truth in a meeting.
How you soften toward another woman instead of judging her.
How you say no with grace.
How you respect your body, in public and in private.

Then let that act become an offering.
Let your everyday life become a prayer.
A blessing.
A quiet revolution.

You are not alone

You may feel like you are walking this path by yourself.
But you are not.

You are part of a lineage of women who are waking up.
Women who are tired of the noise and the pressure.
Women who are choosing to live, lead, and love from a deeper place, a truer place, a place that will sustain us all.

You are not the only one.
You are one of many.
And that is where our power lives.

This is how the new story gets written:
One woman at a time.

One choice at a time.
One sacred return at a time.

And in this return, we rise.

And we remember.

You were born into a story where the feminine was erased.
But now, you are rewriting it.

Not with rage, but with remembrance.
Not with noise, but with truth.

And the women whose wisdom was once buried, they are with you now.

Not as icons on a pedestal.
But as companions. As guides.

You don't need to become them.
You only need to remember:
you were never separate.

Their courage lives in your voice.
Their devotion moves through your breath.
Their knowing rests in your bones.

They are not gone.
They are rising, through you.

And now, *it's your turn.*

Final Invocation
A Call to Devotion

This is not the end.
It's a beginning.
A return.
A turning toward a future that is not yet visible, but already seeded inside you.

You are not who you were when you began this journey.
Maybe you've slowed down.
Perhaps you've softened.
Listened more deeply.
Touched something true, something you hadn't felt in a long time, if ever.

Maybe you've remembered something meaningful.
Not just about wisdom, but about *yourself*.

And maybe, just maybe, you've started to believe that you don't have to keep living, leading, or creating from the places that left you disconnected, depleted, or small.

You've remembered that your truth matters.
That your body is wise.
That your cycles are sacred.

That your way is enough.
That your presence is powerful.

This is the feminine path.
And it doesn't end here.

It continues every time you choose to live from your wholeness.
Every time you honour your inner rhythm instead of the external noise.
Every time you walk away from something that isn't true.
Every time you stand in your knowing, even when it challenges you to your core.

Every time you say:
I remember, and I choose differently now.

Every time you return.

To your inner wisdom.

To truth.

To yourself.

Devotion, not discipline

This path is not a checklist.
It's not another self-improvement project.

It's a *devotion*.

A commitment to keep showing up: for yourself, for the sacred, for your future.

Not perfectly.
Presently.
Wholeheartedly.
With reverence.

Devotion means coming back to yourself again and again, even when you've drifted.

It means trusting that your work, whatever it looks like, isn't about becoming someone new.

It's about *becoming more of who you are.*

Devotion says:
You don't have to know the whole path. You just have to keep saying yes to the next true step.

This is how we walk the feminine way.
With rhythm.
With grace.
With honesty.
With remembrance.

Becoming the future

We are living in a moment between stories.
The old systems are cracking.
The old rules are dissolving.
The old definitions – of success, power, leadership, even womanhood – are being rewritten.

And you are part of that rewriting.

You are not just responding to the future.
You are *shaping* it.

In your choices.
In your rituals.
In your refusals.
In your boundaries.
In your deep inner yes.
In your well held no.

Every time you make that next true choice, you are becoming the future.

A future where power is not domination but discernment.
Where softness is not weakness, but strength.
Where rest is not luxury, but renewal.
Where women do not have to leave themselves behind to rise.

You are not waiting for that future to arrive.
You are already living it.

A prayer for the path

So, what now?

You walk.
You practice.
You remember.
You forget.
You return.

Let your life be an offering.
Let your truth be a blessing.
You let your wisdom shape the world you touch.

Not in grand gestures.
But in the way you hold your own gaze.
The way you speak with integrity.
The way you nourish yourself when no one is watching.
The way you notice the sacred in the everyday.

This is your devotion.

And that, my sister, is enough.

A Blessing for She Who Remembers

May you trust what you know.
May you honour what you feel.
May you rest when you are weary, and rise when you are ready.

May you lead from wholeness.
Create from alignment.
Speak from truth.
Move from love.

May you stop performing and start belonging.
May you stop seeking and start listening.
May you stop proving and start remembering.

You do not need to become someone else.
You do not need to wait for the right moment.
You do not need to be fixed, or perfect, or certain.

You need only to be here.
To be real.
To be you.

You are already the woman you've been waiting for.

Now is the time to live your feminine wisdom.
Now is the time to own your power.
Now is the time for *She Who Remembers*.

Companion Practices for She Who Remembers

You don't have to start over.
You get to spiral deeper.
Carry what you now know,
and let it shape how you live.

This is not more to do.
It's a way to be.
Let each practice hold you.
Let your *life become the altar*.

Living Feminine Wisdom
Companion Practices for She Who Remembers
A sacred invitation to bring the teachings into your life

You've walked the path of remembering.
Through story, truth, and resonance, you've reconnected with the wisdom you never truly lost.

Now, the invitation is simple but profound:
Let this become a way of life.

The practices that follow are not tasks to complete or habits to perfect.
They are invitations – each one a gentle return to your body, your rhythm, your truth.

Move through them one at a time.
Repeat the one you need most.
Let them become ritual, anchoring you, nourishing your soul.

They are not here to add to your to-do list.
They are here to bring you home.

You don't have to remember everything.
You just have to keep returning:

To yourself.

To your wisdom.

To what matters most.

This is what it means to live the feminine way. This is what it means to embody what you now remember.

May these practices support you in your daily return.

Practice One
The First True Step

To accompany Chapter One:
The Threshold

There is a moment when we know:
We cannot keep going the way we have been.
We haven't failed; we're simply being called deeper.
This moment isn't just an ending – *it's an initiation.*
What may feel like collapse can also be the subtle turning of a new cycle.

Enter the threshold

Create a quiet space. Light a candle. Open a window.
Sit where you can feel the earth beneath you or sunlight on your skin.
Let your body soften into the moment.

Close your eyes. Take three slow, conscious breaths.

With each exhale, release the grip of what no longer serves.

Place one hand on your heart, the other on your belly.
Whisper or speak aloud:

"I honour what is ending.
I release what no longer serves me.

I open to what is calling me now."

Let these words settle in your body. Feel them take root.

Reflection and journalling

Let these prompts meet you gently.
Write without editing or rushing. Let your body lead the way.

- What threshold am I standing at right now?

- What am I ready to lay down, with tenderness and truth?

- What am I quietly stepping into, even if I don't have the words for it yet?

- What part of me is whispering: "It's time"?

- What am I clinging to out of comfort or fear?

- What might it feel like to trust the unknown?

If emotions rise, welcome them.
The threshold isn't conceptual, it's alive in you.
Let the page hold your truth.

Embodying the practice

If your body wants to move, try this simple threshold ritual:

- Stand with your feet grounded and steady.
- Imagine a line or threshold on the floor in front of you.
- When you're ready, take one step forward, with intention.
- As you cross, say aloud or inwardly:
  "I cross this threshold with courage and grace."

Pause. Breathe. Feel your whole self on the other side.

Ritual closing

Return to your candle or flame. Let your gaze rest softly on it.
Place one hand on your heart and say, slowly:

*"I trust the path ahead,
Even if I cannot see it yet."*

Blow out the candle or press your palms together in reverence.
Breathe. Pause. Let this be enough.

You've crossed the threshold.
A new way begins.

Practice Two
Your Body's Wisdom

To accompany Chapter Two:
The Wisdom We Forgot

Your body has always known what the world asked you to forget.
She remembers what the mind cannot.
She holds the echoes of truth beneath the noise.

This practice invites you to return to her
with softness and reverence.

Return to the body

Find a quiet, comfortable place.
Lie down or sit supported, with one hand on your heart and the other on your belly.
Close your eyes.

Begin to breathe slowly.
Let your awareness move through your body like a gentle wave –
from the crown of your head, down your face,
your throat, your chest, your belly, your hips, your thighs, your knees,
all the way to your feet.

As you move through each place, pause and silently ask:
What have I been taught to ignore here?
What is waiting for me to remember?

Pause where sensation arises.
Notice what softens. What resists. What speaks.
There is nothing to fix.
Simply witness.

Reflection and journalling

When you're ready, open your journal and meet these questions with curiosity:

- Where in my body do I feel resistance?

- Can I recall a moment when my body spoke to me clearly?

- What sensations have I ignored or overruled in the past?

- What wisdom might be living in the places I've abandoned?

- How might it feel to let my body lead my choices?

- What does remembering feel like in my body, not just in my mind?

Write slowly. Let your body guide your hand.

Embodying the practice

If you feel called to move, try this:

- Stand with your feet grounded.
- Gently sway, stretch, or press into the earth beneath you.
- Place your hands on the parts of your body that want attention.
- You might hum, breathe audibly, or whisper words of gratitude.

You can say:

I hear you.
I trust you.
I remember now.

Let your body move, or rest, as she desires.

Creative ritual

Draw a simple outline of your body in your journal or on a blank page. Using colour, words, or symbols, mark the areas where you feel:

- Memory
- Longing
- Pain
- Pleasure
- Power
- Curiosity
- Resistance

Let it be intuitive. Let it be alive in you.

Ritual closing

Place your hands on your heart and belly.
Close your eyes. Take three slow, steady breaths.

Speak gently:

"I return to the knowing that lives within me."

Stay for a few moments. Let this truth settle into your cells.

Your body knows.
She always has.
And now, *you do too.*

Practice Three
A Remembrance Ritual

To accompany Chapter Three:
She Who Was Silenced

This is a practice of listening.
Of reclaiming.
Of remembering what was buried,
in history, and within you.

You'll need:

- A quiet space

- A candle or a small bowl of water

- A journal or notebook

- *Optional:* a photo, object, or symbol that connects you to your lineage, or a woman you wish to remember

Invite her in

Light your candle or gently place your hand over the bowl of water.
Close your eyes. Breathe deeply into your body.
Feel the steadiness of the ground beneath you.

Let your breath descend:

From your mind to your chest.

From your chest to your belly.

From your belly into the earth.

Let your body remember that it belongs.

Remember her

Call to mind a woman, known or unknown, who represents what was silenced in you.

She might be:

- A historical or mythical figure – like Mary Magdalene, Kali, or Hildegard.
- An ancestor.
- A version of yourself you once abandoned or lost.
- She might even come as a feeling or dream, or an image you can't explain.

Don't force it. Let her come.

When she arrives, imagine her sitting across from you.
Feel her presence.
See her eyes.
Notice what she holds.

Ask gently:
What does she want me to remember?

Then listen.
Not with analysis, but with openness. Not with your mind, but with your heart.

Let her speak, through feeling, image, sensation, or silence.

Reflection and journalling

When you feel ready, open your notebook and begin to write.

- What parts of me have I silenced to be accepted or safe?

- What wisdom am I ready to reclaim?

- Whose voice, within or beyond me, am I listening for now?

- If I could speak one truth I've hidden, what would it be?

Let your words rise without judgement.
Let this be a space of truth, of healing, of reclamation.

Ritual closing

Place your hands on your heart.
Say aloud:

*"You were never gone.
You live in me now.
I remember. And I will not forget."*

Blow out the candle.
Or dip your fingers into the water and anoint your brow, your throat, your heart.

Let this be your vow:

To speak what you were taught to silence.
To walk with those who were erased.
To remember – for yourself, and for all who could not.

Practice Four
What No Longer Fits

To accompany Chapter Four:
When the Old Ways No Longer Hold

There comes a moment when what once carried us begins to crack.
Not because it was wrong, but because we are outgrowing it.
Old systems. Old roles. Old strategies. Old beliefs.
We feel the unravelling, but resist letting go.
Because release can feel like loss, even when it's truth.

This practice is an invitation to lay it down.
With reverence. With honesty. With grace.
So something new can begin to root.

You'll need:

- A quiet space

- A candle or something grounding
  (e.g. a stone, bowl of salt, essential oil)

- Journal or notebook

- Small pieces of paper and a bowl or fire-safe container

- *Optional:* soft instrumental music or a comforting object

Make space for the new

Sit quietly. Light your candle or place your grounding object nearby.
Take three slow breaths into your belly.
Exhale with an audible breath if it feels good.

Place your hands over your heart.
Close your eyes and speak softly:

*"I honour the path that brought me here.
Even though what no longer fits has been part of my becoming, I am ready to lay down what I no longer need."*

Breathe. Let your body soften into the truth of this.

Reflection and journalling

Ask yourself these questions and let the answers rise without effort:

- What belief, role, or rhythm no longer serves who I'm becoming?

- What part of me is exhausted from pretending, performing, or proving?

- What have I outgrown, even if I once loved it?

- What does my body know is ready to be released, even if my mind is still clinging?

- What am I afraid will happen if I let go?

Write freely. Pause if needed. Let your emotions move through you.

Embodying the practice: a release ritual

Take a few small pieces of paper.
For each "old way" you are ready to release, write down a single word or phrase.
(Examples: "Always being available", "Perfection", "Hustle", "Staying small", "Control", "Self-silencing")

When ready, speak each one aloud and place it into your bowl or fire-safe dish.

As you do, say:

*"I release this with gratitude and grace.
It is no longer mine to carry."*

If safe, burn the papers.
Or tear them. Or bury them in the earth later.
Let the ritual be simple, sacred, and complete.

Trust that the energy you've released will compost into wisdom.
You don't need to know how.

Ritual closing

Place your hands on your heart. Breathe deeply.

Say aloud:

*"I release what no longer serves me and I trust what is coming to me.
I walk forward with space to receive."*

Blow out your candle or hold your grounding object close for a few breaths.

You are not lost.
You are in between.
And that too, *is sacred.*

Practice Five
Beneath the Noise

To accompany Chapter Five:
Intuition Is Feminine Intelligence

Intuition isn't something you earn.

It's something you remember, your divine natural intelligence.

It lives in your body and breath, in your subtle awareness.

This practice invites you to return to it gently and honestly, without the need for performance.

You'll need:

- A quiet space
- Journal or notebook
- A candle, oil, or touchstone
- *Optional:* a small object that symbolises inner knowing (e.g. a stone, feather, talisman)

Tune the inner frequency

Light your candle or hold your touchstone.
Sit quietly. Let your breath deepen.

Place one hand on your heart, one on your belly.
Close your eyes and whisper:

*"I am willing to listen, even if the voice is quiet.
I listen now, even if I've ignored it before."*

Let yourself fully arrive in your body.
Feel your feet. Your spine. The rhythm of your breath.
You are not here to analyse.
You are here to feel.

Reflection and journalling

Take your journal and respond to the following invitations:

- When have I felt a quiet knowing, even if I couldn't explain it?

- Describe a time when my body said no when my mind said yes.

- What signals have I overridden or dismissed in the past?

- What is one way I could follow my inner knowing this week?

- What gets in the way of trusting myself?

- What helps me come back?

Let the answers rise without pressure.

Truth often arrives in whispers.

Embodying the practice: yes and no scan

This is a practice of energetic alignment.

- Stand or sit upright. Close your eyes.

- Say the word "yes" out loud. Slowly. Three times.

- Notice what happens in your body. Expansion? Softness? Tingling?

- Now say "no" three times.

- Again, notice. Tightening? Pulling back? Numbness?

Now try this with two small questions you're currently holding:

(e.g. "Do I want to rest tonight?" or "Is this project aligned?")
Say each one aloud.
Feel the body's immediate response, not the mind's story.

This is how we begin to listen:
Not through logic, but through sensation.

Ritual closing

Place your hand on the part of your body where truth lives today.
Say aloud:

*"I trust what I feel.
Even when it's quiet.
Even when no one else sees it.
My knowing is enough."*

Blow out your candle. Or press your touchstone to your heart.

You already know.
You always have.
Now, you *begin to listen.*

Practice Six
The Power of Presence

*To accompany Chapter Six:
Presence Over Performance*

You weren't born to perform.
You were born to belong, to yourself, to the moment, to what's real.

This practice is a soft return to presence.
To the part of you that doesn't need to prove, please, or perfect.

You'll need:

- A quiet space

- Journal or notebook

- A candle, essential oil, or grounding object (e.g. a stone, flower, or textile)

- *Optional:* mirror, or a photo of yourself as a child

Return to here

Sit comfortably. Light your candle or hold your grounding object.
Take three slow, steady breaths into your belly.
Feel your body settle. Notice what's here.

Place a hand over your heart or your solar plexus and whisper:

"I do not need to perform to be worthy.
I am allowed to be here, just as I am."

Breathe. Let these words land. Let your face soften.

If using a mirror or photo, gently meet your gaze. Notice who's there when you're not trying to be anything but you.

Reflection and journalling

Take your journal and explore:

- Where in my life do I feel like I'm performing or perfecting?

- What am I afraid will happen if I stop?

- When do I feel most present and real?

- What helps me return to myself when I feel off centre?
- What does presence feel like in my body right now?

No need to fix or solve. Let this be a moment of honest witnessing.

Embodying the practice: a pause ritual

This is a micro-practice to use anytime you feel yourself slipping into performance.

- Pause whatever you're doing.
- Drop your shoulders. Soften your jaw. Place your hand on your body.

    Ask silently:
    "Am I here?"
    "Am I with myself?"

- Take one conscious breath and exhale fully.
- Say (out loud or silently):
    "I choose presence, not performance."

Try this in real time, before you speak, type, reply or rush, or anytime you feel the mask creeping in.

Ritual closing

Sit in silence for a few more breaths.

Say gently:

*"I do not need to earn my place.
My presence is enough."*

Blow out the candle or press your palms together in reverence.

You don't have to prove anything.
You get to belong.
This is the power of your presence. And it is enough.

Practice Seven
Coming Home to Yourself

To accompany Chapter Seven:
Coming Home to Wholeness

You were never meant to live in pieces.
Your wholeness is not a future goal. It's a present truth, waiting to be remembered, felt, and lived.

This practice is an invitation to come home to yourself.
To gather what's been scattered.
To move from fragmented to integrated.
To live from the centre, not the edges.

You'll need:

- A quiet space
- Journal or notebook
- A candle or grounding object (e.g. a stone, blanket, or something soft)
- *Optional:* a small bowl or token to represent your wholeness

Return to centre

Light your candle. Wrap yourself in something soft if it helps you feel held.
Take three full breaths, in through your nose, out through your mouth, letting the exhale be an audible sigh.

Place both hands on your heart and speak gently:

*"I do not need to do more to be more.
I am already whole."*

Let yourself arrive fully in the moment. Let your body soften.

Reflection and journalling

Settle in with your notebook and respond to the following:

- What parts of me have I left behind in the name of success, survival, or acceptance?

- Where have I split myself to meet expectations?

- What does wholeness *feel like* in my body?

- What am I craving more of? Less of?

- How would my life look if I lived from the belief: *I am already whole*?

Let this be a space for gentle reclamation, not judgement.

Embodying the practice: a gathering ritual

Use this practice when you feel fragmented or overextended.

Sit or stand with your feet grounded.

Open your arms wide, palms open.

Slowly move your hands inward toward your heart, as if gathering the pieces of yourself back to your centre. Do this six or more times.

Let your hands rest on your heart.

Say softly:

*"I call myself home.
Every part of me is welcome.
I am whole."*

Repeat as often as you need. Let this movement become a felt prayer.

Ritual closing

Hold your grounding object or bowl (if using).
Place it in front of you, as a symbol of your wholeness.

Speak aloud:

*"I release the need to prove or perform.
I choose to live from wholeness and from my truth, my centre and my enoughness."*

Blow out your candle or close your eyes and rest for a few moments.
Let your breath be the exhale of return.

You don't need to become more.
You need only to remember:
*You are already whole.
You are already home.*

Practice Eight
Returning to the Body

*To accompany Chapter Eight:
Embodiment Is Power*

Your body is not a project.
Not a problem to be fixed.
Not something to be perfected or managed.
It is sovereign ground.
And this practice is your invitation to return to it with grace.

You'll need:

- A quiet space
- Journal or notebook
- *Optional:* a mirror, blanket, oil or lotion, or music that connects you to your body

Re-inhabit your body

Find a comfortable seat or lie down.
Close your eyes. Place one hand on your heart, the other on your belly.
Take three deep, slow breaths.
Feel gravity holding you. Let your body soften.

Speak softly aloud:

"I am not separate from my body.
She is not in my way.
She is the way."

Stay here for a moment, letting that truth land.

Reflection and journalling

Open your journal and write freely in response to the following:

- How have I been taught to view or treat my body?

- What parts of my body have I judged, ignored, or abandoned?

- What does reverence for my body look like in action? What does it feel like?

- Where do I feel most alive, most true, most powerful in my body?

- What is one way I can come into deeper relationship with her?

Let the pen move from honesty, not performance. This is not about fixing, it's about listening.

Embodying the practice: a reclamation ritual

Choose one of the following. Or follow your own impulse:

Option 1: Movement

- Put on music that invites you to move slowly and with ease.

- Let your body lead, no mirrors, no one watching. Just be here now.

- Ask: *How does power move through me?*

Option 2: Anointing

- Use oil or lotion. Slowly massage your arms, belly, or heart.

- As you touch each part, say:
  "This is sacred."
  "This belongs."
  "This is mine."

Option 3: Mirror Gaze

- Stand or sit in front of a mirror. Look into your own eyes or at your full form.

- Whisper a blessing:
  "I see you."
  "You are not too much. You are enough. You are safe."

Let the ritual be quiet and real. Even a few moments can shift everything.

Ritual closing

Wrap yourself in a blanket or simply place your hands on your body.
Say aloud:

*"I live in my body.
And my body is sacred and where my power lives."*

Stay for a few breaths. Let this moment be alive in you.

You are not here to be disconnected.
You are here to belong.
To feel.
To remember that your body is not the barrier to your wisdom.
She is the portal to your power.

Practice Nine
Honouring Your Seasons

*To accompany Chapter Nine:
The Wisdom of Seasons*

You are not meant to bloom all year.
You are not meant to be linear in a world made of cycles.
This practice is a quiet return to rhythm.
To the wisdom of where you are, not where you think you should be.

You'll need:

- A quiet space

- Journal or notebook

- A candle or object from nature (e.g. a stone, leaf, feather, flower)

- *Optional:* a moon calendar or journal from the past month

Step into sacred time

Light your candle or hold your chosen object.
Sit comfortably. Take three slow, spacious breaths.

Whisper aloud or silently:

"I honour the season I am in.
Even if I don't yet understand it.
Even if it's not what I wanted or expected.
Even if the world tells me I should be somewhere else."

Let your body settle into the honesty of this moment.

Reflection and journalling

Open your notebook. Gently explore:

- What does the current season of my soul feel like – winter, spring, summer, or autumn?

- What is this season asking of me? Slowness? Creation? Clarity? Stillness? Expansion?

- Where am I trying to push when I need to pause?

- Where am I holding back when I feel the urge to rise?

- What would change if I trusted this cycle instead of resisting it?

Optional: Look back over your past month: what patterns or rhythms emerged? What truths have been repeating themselves?

Embodying the practice: seasonal mapping

Draw a circle on a blank page. Divide it into four quadrants:

- **Winter** – Rest, reflection, endings
- **Spring** – Vision, new energy, beginning
- **Summer** – Expression, fullness, visibility
- **Autumn** – Harvest, boundary, completion

Ask:

Where am I now?
Where am I headed?
What does my energy need in this moment?

Notice if you are in different seasons for different aspects of your life, i.e. relationships, career, spiritual life. Mark your places in the turning of the wheel, no pressure or judgement, just intuition.
Let this visual reminder honour your rhythm, not the world's pace or projection.

Ritual closing

Return to your breath.
Hold your nature object or place your hands on your body.

Say aloud:

*"My rhythm is right for me.
I am exactly where I need to be."*

Blow out the candle or simply sit in stillness.
Let the wisdom of your season hold you.

You are not behind or broken.
You are seasonal.
Let that knowing be enough.

Practice Ten
Your Inner Compass

*To accompany Chapter Ten:
Trusting What You Know*

You've been taught to seek the answers outside of yourself.
To wait for a map, a mentor, or a moment of certainty.
But your wisdom is already here.
It lives in your body.
In your longings.
In the part of you that whispers, *this is true*, even when you don't know why.

This practice is a return to that knowing.

You'll need:

- A quiet space

- Journal or notebook

- A candle or grounding object (e.g. a stone, feather, photo)

Meet the knower within

Light your candle or hold your grounding object.

Place one hand on your heart, the other on your belly.

Take three slow, spacious breaths.
Whisper or say aloud:

*"I already know.
Even if the voice is quiet.
Even if the world doesn't understand.
I trust what is true for me."*

Feel the words move through your body. Notice where they land.

Reflection and journalling

Answer these invitations slowly. Let your body guide the pace:

- What decision, situation, or feeling have I been overthinking?

- Beneath the doubt, what do I already know?

- Where might I be pretending not to know, because knowing would require change?

- What does trust feel like in my body?
  What does betrayal feel like?

- What would it look like to believe myself today?

Optional:
Write a letter from your inner knowing to your thinking mind. Let her speak clearly, even if it's just one line.

Embodying the practice: alignment scan

This is a deeper step from the yes/no scan in Practice Five. Instead of only feeling the baseline, you apply it to a choice you're holding.

- Sit or stand comfortably. Close your eyes.

- Say the word "yes" three times aloud. Pause. Notice how your body responds.

- Say the word "no" three times aloud. Pause. Notice again.

Now, bring in a real situation or choice:

- Speak it aloud in the form of a statement.
  "Staying in this job."
  "Launching this idea."
  "Taking the rest I need."

- Notice what happens in your body immediately, before your mind explains. Expansion? Tightness? Energy? Fatigue?

- Write down what you discovered.

This is how your inner compass speaks: through sensation, not logic.

Ritual closing

Place your hand over your heart. Breathe.

Say aloud:

*"My knowing is enough.
I trust myself, even in the unknown.
I will follow what feels true."*

Blow out your candle or sit in stillness for a few moments.

You don't need another answer.
You need to trust the one already inside you.
This is your wisdom.
And it's waiting to be lived.

Practice Eleven
Living From Within

To accompany Chapter Eleven:
Living the Feminine Way

The feminine way isn't a lifestyle trend.
It's a way of listening.
Of orienting your life around truth, not performance.
Around rhythm, not rigidity.
Around devotion, not discipline.

This practice is an invitation to remember what that looks like in your life, in this moment.

You'll need:

- A quiet space

- Journal or notebook

- *Optional:* candle, tea, music, or soft lighting to create sacred space

Enter the feminine within

Close your eyes.
Place one hand on your belly, the other on your heart.
Take three slow breaths. Inhale deeply, exhale fully.

Whisper inwardly or aloud:

"I choose to live from within.
To follow what feels real.
To let rhythm, ritual, and relationship guide me home."

Let your shoulders soften.

Let your breath deepen.

Let this be a beginning.

Reflection and journalling

Let these questions guide you. There is no rush.
No right answer. Only honesty.

Rhythm

- What is the current rhythm of my days? Does it reflect what I most need?

- Where am I rushing? Where am I resisting rest?

- What would it feel like to let my energy lead my schedule?

Ritual

- What rituals already live in my life? *(Consider how you wake up, eat, transition between tasks, prepare for rest.)*
- Which moments feel special, even in their simplicity?
- What is one small ritual I can create or deepen, just for me?

Relationship

- Where am I feeling connection in my life right now?
- Where am I feeling disconnected, overextended, or out of sync?
- Who helps me return to myself? Who drains me or pulls me away?

Finally, ask yourself:

What would it look like to live more honestly?

More slowly?

More softly?

Write what rises.

Embodying the practice: a feminine way to check-in

Choose a typical day of your week.
Without judgement, make two simple lists:

- How I currently move through my day
- How I want to move through my day (the feminine way)

For example:

- *Current:* Wake up, check phone, rush into tasks.
- *Feminine:* Wake slowly, check in with my body, begin with breath or gratitude.

This isn't about perfection. It's not a prescription. It's a reorientation.

Choose one small shift to try tomorrow. Tune in to how it makes you feel.

Ritual closing

Close your journal. Place your hands on your heart. Breathe.

Say aloud:

*"I do not need to perform this way of life.
I become it – breath by breath, choice by choice.
I live from within."*

Blow out your candle. Sip your tea.

Or simply sit in silence and stillness.

Let this moment seal your devotion.

You don't need to do more.
You simply need to listen more deeply.
To your rhythm.
To your wisdom.
To the way your life wants to be lived.

Practice Twelve
Leading From Your Centre

To accompany Chapter Twelve:
Leading From Your True Self

Leadership isn't a role.
It's a relationship with your truth and your values.
This practice is a return to that relationship.
It invites you to lead not from pressure or
performance, but from alignment, authenticity,
and deep self-trust.

You'll need:

- A quiet moment and space
- Journal or notebook
- *Optional:* candle or grounding object to anchor intention

Anchor your leadership energy

Close your eyes.
Place one hand on your belly and one on your heart.
Take three long, slow breaths. Let your mind soften
and your body arrive.

Whisper softly:

"I choose to lead from within, from my values and my truth. I lead from my whole self."

Let this settle in your body. Feel what shifts.

Reflection and journalling

This is where you meet your leadership differently – not as role-play, but as real embodiment.

- Where am I leading (in life, work, family, community) right now?

- Where do I feel most aligned in how I show up, and where do I feel performative, disconnected, or overextended?

- What part of me have I been hiding in order to be acceptable, impressive, or safe?

- What does leadership feel like in my body when I'm truly being myself?

- How would I lead if I trusted that my authentic self was enough?

Let your words be raw and honest. You're not writing to impress, you're writing to return.

Embodying the practice: reclaiming your voice

Stand or sit tall. Close your eyes.
Take a few breaths, then speak aloud (in a whisper or full voice):

"I lead with... [insert your truth]."

Examples:

- "I lead with integrity."
- "I lead with clarity and boundaries."
- "I lead with softness and strength."
- "I lead with honesty, even when it shakes me."

Let the words rise from your body, not your mind.

Repeat this phrase until it feels like a vow.

A leadership inventory

Create a two-column list in your journal:
Where I'm Leading from Performance
vs
Where I'm Leading from Truth and Alignment

Look at meetings, decisions, relationships, or choices you're navigating.

This is about awareness, not self-judgement.
Where can you shift even ten per cent towards deeper alignment?

Then answer:

What's one micro-shift I can make this week to lead more honestly – from my body, my values, or my truth?

Write it. Circle it. Commit to it.

Ritual closing

Return your hands to your body.
Close your eyes and say:

"I do not have to lead like others.

I lead like me.

With clarity, integrity, authenticity and truth.

And that is enough.

I am enough."

Blow out your candle, take a breath, or move gently back into your day.

You don't have to wear the mask.
You don't have to perform power.

You already have it.
And now, *you get to lead from who you truly are.*

Practice Thirteen
Meeting the Divine Feminine

To accompany Chapter Thirteen:
Walking With the Goddess

You are not meant to worship Her from a distance.
You are meant to remember Her within you.
To walk with Her. To listen for Her.
To let Her many faces awaken your own.

This is a practice of sacred remembering.
A quiet encounter. A personal initiation.

Open the sacred door

Create a space that feels intentional.
Light a candle or sit in soft natural light.
You may wish to place a symbol, stone, or image
on a small cloth or table before you – anything that
reminds you of the sacred.

Close your eyes.
Place one hand on your heart, the other on your belly.
Take five slow, deep breaths.

Whisper:

"I open to the face of the Divine Feminine I most need today. I remember that She is not outside of me, She lives in me."

Let silence follow. Tune in.

Invocation and visualisation

With your eyes closed, invite the Goddess to appear. She may come as:

- An archetype: Mother, Warrior, Mystic, Crone
- A known goddess: Saraswati, Kali, Brigid, Quan Yin
- A sensation: fire in your belly, calm in your heart
- A memory, a word, an image, a breath

Trust what comes. Don't force. Simply allow.

If nothing comes right away, say softly:

"Show me who I most need to meet."

Stay with Her for a few minutes.

Let Her speak, not in words necessarily, but in vibration.
Feel Her. Welcome Her. Receive Her.

Reflection and journalling

When you are ready, open your journal and write:

- Who came in? What did She feel like? What did She offer me?

- What part of me does She mirror or awaken?

- Where in my life do I need Her energy right now?

- What is one way I can honour Her?

Don't rush. Let this be a conversation across time and lineage.

Optional embodiment practice

Stand and let your body move the way it wants to move.
Does She want to sway? To be still? To stretch? To ground?
Let yourself become Her, even for a moment.
Let your body speak Her language.

Ritual closing

Return to the candle or symbol you placed at the beginning.
Place both hands over your heart.

Say aloud:

*"You were never gone.
I remember you now.
And I will carry you forward
through how I live, how I lead, how I love, how I remember."*

Blow out the candle. Touch your heart.
Feel the sacred settle into the ordinary.

She is not elsewhere. She is here.
In you. As you. With you.
And when you remember Her,
you remember yourself.

Practice Fourteen
The Sacred Circle

*To accompany Chapter Fourteen:
The Sacred Thread*

This practice is a remembering that your becoming is for you, but not only for you.
Every aligned step you take is a thread in the larger weave.
Every act of reclamation, rest, or truth-telling creates space for someone else to do the same.

This is a practice of soulful ripple-making – beginning within, and flowing outward, gently and powerfully.

Step into the circle

Find a quiet space. Sit comfortably. Light a candle if you wish.
Close your eyes. Place both hands over your heart.
Take five slow, grounding breaths. Feel your body rise and fall.

Now whisper:

*"I honour the women who came before me.
I walk for those who could not.*

*I rise for all who are still finding their way.
May my remembering ripple outward."*

Let yourself feel connected to those with you, past, present, and future.

Lineage and legacy reflection

Open your journal. Let this be a spacious inquiry.

- Whose stories do I carry in my bones, even if they've never been spoken?

- What am I healing, not just for myself, but for the generations before and after me?

- What does sacred activism look like in my daily life?

- How do I want to influence the world through my actions?

- What future do I want my daughters, sisters, or wider community to inherit, and how am I helping shape it?

If emotions rise, pause and breathe. You are not holding this alone.
You are part of something vast and ancient and wise.

Embodying the ripple

Stand or move gently in your space. With your hands over your heart, speak aloud:

*"My being is a prayer.
My choices are offerings, and my life is part of the great feminine weaving of our sacred return."*

Optional:

- Take a slow walk outside, barefoot if possible.

- With each step, repeat softly:
  "I walk with them. I rise with them. I remember for us all."

Let the earth receive your prayer and devotion.

A simple offering ritual

Choose one small act to complete today as a conscious offering to the collective:

- Reach out to a woman who may need encouragement.

- Rest without apology and let others see it.

- Speak a truth, gently and clearly.

- Leave flowers somewhere unexpected.

- Donate, support, or show up where your energy is needed.

- Send love and healing to someone or somewhere that needs it.

Before or after your act, return to stillness and say:

"This is for the world I want to live in.
This is for the women rising with me.
This is for the future already forming."

Closing blessing

Place one hand on your heart, one on your belly.
Take one deep breath for yourself.
One for your lineage.
One for the collective.

Then say, slowly:

"May my life be an offering.
May my energy be a blessing.
May my remembering help us all rise."

Blow out your candle. Bow to yourself.

You are not alone.
You are one of many.
And *together, we rise.*

Keep Returning
A letter for She Who Remembers

By now, you know: *this was never just a book.*
It was a call. A remembering. A return.
A quiet revolution, seeded in your own heart.

You've walked through stories and silence,
questions and truths, some familiar, some forgotten,
some newly revealed.

You are not who you were when you began.
Not because you've become someone new, but because you've come home to more of who you've always been.

This journey is not about arriving.
It's about continuing, gently, honestly, in rhythm with your own being.
It's about walking your own way, and trusting in your own path.

And yes, you will forget.
You will get caught in the noise again.
You will doubt, perform, override.
You will feel tired, small, out of sync.
And still, even then, you can return.

So keep listening.
Keep tending.

Keep softening.
Keep choosing truth over expectation.
Keep offering yourself grace when the world demands more than you want to give.

Above all, *keep returning.*
To your body.
To your breath.
To your knowing.
To the woman you already are, and the one you are still becoming.

Because you are the wisdom.
You are the way.
You are the gift and the magic that the world needs.

You are *She Who Remembers.*

With love and reverence,
Megan

A Final Blessing

When you are ready, close the book.
Place your hands over your heart.
Take three deep breaths.

And say aloud or softly within:

I remember.
I return.
I rise.

Let that be your prayer.
Let your life be the practice.

She Who Remembers Circles

Weaving the Thread Together
An Invitation to Gather

This book was never meant to be read alone.

It was written in devotion, for you, and for the many women who are waking up beside you.
The ones you know.
And the ones you've never met.
The ones who are remembering, just like you, that we were never meant to walk this path by ourselves.

There is something alchemical that happens when women come together with intention.
Not to fix each other.
Not to perform.
But to remember, through story, silence, resonance, and presence.

This is your invitation to gather.

Not as a book club in the usual sense.
But as a *circle of remembrance.*
A space to reflect. To feel. To witness. To return.

You can begin simply:

- Invite a few women who are also longing for something deeper.

- Light a candle.

- Read one chapter aloud, or one of the Companion Practices.

- Let each woman speak what's rising, or rest in the quiet if no words come.

- Let the circle hold what is present.

There is no wrong way to do this.
Only your way.
Rooted in reverence.
Held in honesty.
Guided by the wisdom that is rising in each of you.

You might gather once a week for fourteen weeks, one chapter at a time.
You might move slower. Or spiral back again.
You might create rituals, bring objects for the altar, or share a meal.

You might have a tea ceremony or a glass of wine.
You might cry. You might laugh. You might find your voice in a way you never have before.

What matters most is not the format.
It's the *intention:*
To gather in a soulful space.
To practice remembrance.

To celebrate the feminine, in yourself, and in each other.

Because when women come together in this way, something ancient is restored.
The thread is rewoven.
The remembering deepens.
And a new story begins to take root, not in isolation, but in sisterhood.

Let this book be the beginning of something more.
Something sacred.
Something shared.
Something remembered.

Let this be the thread we weave, together.
Let this be *our collective return*.

She Who Remembers Circle Guide

If you feel called to gather women in this way, I've created a free **She Who Remembers Circle Guide** to support you.

It offers a simple soulful structure for your gathering, with guidance for opening and closing your time together, creating a supportive space, and moving through shared reflection drawn from the chapters and companion practices.

The guide isn't a script, just a gentle framework you can use as a guide, especially if you're hosting for the first time or want a little clarity as you begin.

Take what feels true, leave what doesn't, and shape it in a way that suits your circle.

You can download your free guide at: megandallacamina.com/circle

I trust this will support the circles you create, the conversations that unfold, and the women who gather with you. May you each remember your wisdom and power.

ABOUT THE AUTHOR

Megan Dalla-Camina is a best-selling author, award-winning teacher, and PhD researcher in women's spirituality. Her work is dedicated to women's sacred return home to themselves.

She is the founder of *Women Rising*™ and *The Feminine Wisdom Codes*™, guiding women around the world to awaken their feminine wisdom and embody their true power. For more than two decades, Megan has worked at the intersection of women's leadership, empowerment, and spirituality – bridging science, spirit, and sādhanā.

A long-time student and teacher of yoga, meditation, and ancient wisdom traditions, Megan is an initiate of Himalayan Tantric-Vedantic lineage and a lifelong seeker.

She lives by the sea in Australia with her family, where she writes, teaches, and continues her research on feminine wisdom and awakening.

Connect with Megan:
On social media @megandallacamina
and at megandallacamina.com

www.ingramcontent.com/pod-product-compliance
Lightning Source LLC
LaVergne TN
LVHW031539060526
838200LV00056B/4572